GROWING

INTO THE

GRAY

GROWING
INTO THE
GRAY

Reflections on Transforming
Trauma for Women
and the World

L AURIE L EE D AVIDSON

AMPLE WAVES PRESS
San Diego, California, United States

AMPLE WAVES PRESS
San Diego, CA

Paperback ISBN: 979-8-9861226-0-1
eBook ISBN: 979-8-9861226-1-8

Library of Congress Control Number: 2022911636

Book cover and interior design by Erin Seaward-Hiatt
Editorial production by kn literary

www.amplewavespress.com

Printed in the United States of America

For Gloria—therapist, healer, spiritual midwife—who gave me a second chance at this amazing life and helped me retrieve my voice.

No mud, no lotus.

—*Thich Nhat Hanh*

The only way out is through.

—*Gabrielle Roth*

CONTENTS

INTRODUCTION

When you can't go far, you go deep.
—*Brother David Steindl-Rast*

Brother David's words rang so true in my life during the many months of the COVID-19 pandemic, he might as well have been speaking specifically about me. Of course, he wasn't, and many of you reading this book may also resonate with his sentiment just as strongly as I, but I have gone ahead and adopted his words as my subtitle for this period in my personal history. You see, by the dawn of 2020, things really seemed to be falling into place for me. At sixty-one years old, I was well over four years into a profound personal awakening process, and I now had a new outlook on myself, a new sense of purpose in life, even a new vocation on the horizon. I was set to go far, literally, with extensive plans for the coming year that would take me to distant places as I checked off the remaining prerequisite classes and workshops that I needed to enroll in 5Rhythms (5R) teacher training. I smile ruefully now at the optimism on display back then, when, on Valentine's Day, I exchanged emails with one of the instructors in which we remarked together on the recent synchronicities of my path and how delightful it was that the "Universe had aligned."

Just under a month later, the Universe revealed that it had a completely different plan than the one we thought we'd understood. COVID hit with full force—officially declared a global pandemic by the World Health Organization on March 11— and soon I could go absolutely nowhere, confined instead to my home under a governmental shelter-in-place order, dismayed as I watched my carefully plotted course begin to crumble in the face of travel bans, event cancellations, program shutdowns, and all the rest. However, like perhaps for most people, it took a while for the full import of this shared crisis to sink in for me, so it wasn't until several weeks into the oddity of quarantine that I finally came to grips with what I'd lost: my future, or rather my picture of how it was going to unfold.

I came to this realization one morning through 5Rhythms itself, a type of freeform mindful dance of inestimable therapeutic value that I'll describe more fully later in the book. Home alone, in a space I'd cleared of furniture to provide a makeshift dance floor, I began to move to some music my local teacher had prerecorded, tuning into my body. I felt a tight ache in my chest, telling me that my heart was breaking, and a lump the size of a fist choking my throat, telling me that my soul was sorrowing. Knowing from experience that it's best to give these discomforts expression, to get them up and out, I took a deep breath, relaxed my defenses against them, and leaned into the sensations. That simple permission allowed them to melt into hot flowing tears and erupt into husky shaking sobs, and I kept my body company through what it needed to let go of, moving with the music and the energy the whole time. The venting session was brief but intense, and as the powerful grief subsided, I felt blessedly warm and buoyant, my chest loose, my throat clear. I danced the rest of the session with a lighter heart.

Shortly after this cleansing experience, when I shared with one of my 5R mentors how I'd realized and released my pain over losing my plans, she said to me, "Good for you. It was never about checking off prerequisites, anyway. It's always been about the journey." Her statement affirmed what I knew to be true through my experience: By allowing myself to mourn my imagined future in an embodied way, I'd opened myself up to fully inhabiting my present reality. I'd let go of clinging to dance training and could now ask myself what else I felt drawn to. To answer that question, I started to do what my dear brother-in-law calls Mister Dogging It, after a beloved children's book character. I followed my nose and my instincts, without a plan.

They shortly led me to writing. Initially, I decided to work on what I thought would be a blog post—the first of many perhaps. I liked the original piece I wrote and shared it with my husband who surprised me with his enthusiastic response. I then passed it by my adult son, an accomplished writer not afraid to tell his mother exactly what he thinks, and he unexpectedly seconded my husband's excitement. Because I immensely enjoyed the writing process itself and felt spurred on by such affirming feedback (though from an admittedly narrow and inarguably biased pool of critics), I began to write more and more. I spent hours of my quarantine time seated in front of my laptop, fingers tapping furiously, transported into a state of absorption and flow.

When I had several pieces finished, I decided it was time to start posting. Even though I'm reasonably tech savvy for someone of my generation, having had an online business presence earlier in my working life, for some reason my attempts to create a website this time proved infuriating and unfruitful. I attempted several times to make it work, trying to power through the roadblocks I encountered, my frustration mounting with each unsuccessful effort. When

I found myself uncharacteristically railing against the "inept hosting site," the "convoluted software," the "blasted internet" itself, I finally woke up to the message my subconscious—maybe the Universe?—was trying to send me: *Let the blog idea go, Laurie.* Since I was loving the writing itself, I decided to keep going with that, and as I did, it slowly dawned on me that perhaps I was crafting a book.

During the ensuing weeks of furious creating, I opened up about my work to a writer friend, and she encouraged me to run with it. So, I wholeheartedly gave myself over to the process, which began to consume me. It took over my life. I'd be washing the dishes and—boom!—a compelling idea of something to write would come to me out of the blue. I'd dry my hands and run to scribble it down so I wouldn't forget. This same sort of "download" occurred at other random times, like when I was doing the laundry or taking a walk. I started carrying a pad and pen with me everywhere. There were scraps of paper all over my house. On the day I found myself with one hand on the steering wheel and the other trying to jot down something while driving, I began to seriously doubt my own sanity. What was happening to me? Was this some kind of unholy obsession?

Another check-in with my writer friend helped calm me immensely and alleviate my fears. I wasn't going crazy. She assured me that the odd experiences and unfamiliar behaviors cropping up in my life were simply signs that I was becoming a writer, experiencing a creative opening. "How lovely for you. Embrace it," she said. So, I did. During the next twelve months, I felt drawn to write about the journey of transformation I'd begun in 2015 and its positive significance for my life because the wider world now seemed to echo it—and the need for its important lessons—so very loudly. While I looked outward at my planet and fellow inhabitants struggling mightily, I also looked within, finding parallels and convergences, and wrote about the understandings and insights that came to me through this dual looking. The work of expressing myself with words proved to be personally helpful—even healing—a truly beneficial way to spend the hours in lock-down, a way to make sense not only of my own life but also of what was happening here on Earth at this watershed moment. As I proceeded, I also wondered if there was more to it. Was this strictly a personal practice, meant only for me, or was I meant to share it? Might others benefit from reading about my experiences and my reflections?

The phrase "Your pain is your purpose"—a message Seane Corn received from her beloved therapist and wrote about in her book *Revolution of the Soul*—began resounding in my head because getting in touch with long-buried anguish had been at the core of my transformation. I'd set my feet on the 5Rhythms training path before COVID struck precisely because I'd wanted to learn how to share a movement modality that had brought me the balm of healing. Having opened myself up to great pain and found a way to transmute it through the dance, I felt it was part of my purpose in life to offer others the opportunity to move through their challenges in a similar way. A responsibility almost. I could pay it forward, in gratitude for the immeasurable gift of renewal I'd received. That opportunity was gone for now, but perhaps I'd stumbled upon another way to embody Seane's resonant words—by putting my own down on the pages of a book.

So, that's what this is. A book of essays I wrote—one flowing into the next, Mister Dogging It style—during the first twelve months of the COVID pandemic, a deep dive into the meaning of life, love, and well-being, both personal and collective, prompted by pain. It contains reflections on the challenges and joys experienced, and on the learnings and questions raised, during my healing from trau-ma—a healing that began before the virus emerged and continued as the scourge unfolded. Reflections penned, or rather typed, while the world itself experienced trauma on a massive scale and in multiple arenas.

Let me be clear that these reflections tell *my* story of healing and do not represent a prescription. I am not mapping an ideal trajectory. I am neither recommending nor dismissing any specific treatments or modalities. I am not a scientist, doctor, therapist, counselor, or expert in any way on the subject matter of trauma. What I am, however, is a trauma survivor. Actually, I'm more than that. I'm a trauma thriver, if you will, an embodiment of post-traumatic growth (PTG), as it's called in psychology—a phenomenon first identified by Richard Tedeschi and Lawrence Calhoun in the 1990s, and the subject of almost as much study and research as post-traumatic stress disorder (PTSD), though not as widely disseminated. Through the work of recovery, which for me was emphatically somatic and launched me into PTG, I've been given a second chance at life. And if sharing my story can help anyone else, then I must tell it.

So, trauma and the body are my lenses, and in this book, I look through them at many aspects of what it means to me to be a woman, a woman in her later years, a woman wanting something more out of life, a woman desiring greater wholeness for herself and humanity, a woman attempting to make meaning out of her one precious span of existence. If you are aware that trauma in some way bent your life out of shape, too, and that's the reason you're reading this book, I'm so glad you're here. I can tell you from personal experience that transformation and growth beyond that painful reality are possible. Life can become better than you might ever have imagined.

If that's not the case, if you haven't embraced the idea that trauma pertains to your life, please don't let any discomfort with the word stop you from reading on. Too often, people associate it with horrendous things that happen, out there, to others, when it's just code for the human experience—on a continuum, certainly, but shared by all. If you are a woman "of a certain age" who has ever felt even one moment's dissatisfaction with the way things are in your life, or in the world around you, I invite you to continue. You might just discover something helpful. If you're younger and curious, my invitation extends to you too. It seems to me that we women need to build bridges across the years to each other, now more than ever. If you're a man or if you gender-identify more fluidly than binarily and are still intrigued, please feel free to proceed as well. I suspect there might be a morsel or two in here for you too. After all, I touch on embodiment, love, racism, family, intimate partnership, work, sexuality, citizenship—common elements across much of the human experience.

Regardless of who you understand yourself to be at this moment and what the reasons are that brought you here, I hope you find something in these musings to stir your curiosity, inspire your journey, get you thinking, warm your heart, piss you off, start your questioning—move you somehow. In 2020, via a microscopic pathogen, Mother Nature issued a very loud and public call for movement—away from ways of being, structures, and priorities that are no longer working and toward new ones that serve, nurture, and sustain. In it, I heard echoes of the more personal call to transform I had received a few years earlier, and through writing this book, I discovered that they might just be one and the same, and that it might just be—in some way—for everyone. Read on and see if you agree.

You might not, and that's fine. It's not important we agree. What is important is you allow yourself to stay open to what arises within you while reading this book. So, I invite you to lovingly greet every thought, emotion, sensation, memory, state, longing, whatever bubbles up. And I invite you to notice not just moments of delight and connection with the story but also moments of defensiveness, moments of dissociation or disconnection from it. See if you can welcome it all. Especially, perhaps, any challenging feelings that might get triggered, like fear, anger, or shame. Despite what our culture may say, they are our dear friends, often key signposts revealing something deep inside us that needs our tender attention. May your internal experience of my words illuminate the important turning points in your own life, those already navigated (lord knows, COVID alone created plenty for each of us) or those still on the horizon, and show you how your path forward into post-traumatic growth might look similar to, or very different from, mine. It's all the raw material for your own unique healing story, whether you ever choose to write it down or not.

I find it ironic, but if the pandemic hadn't happened, I might never have found my own voice on the page. I was so busy pursuing one path—willing to go far across the globe to achieve it—that I would not have slowed down and gone deep inside enough to discover another. I didn't enter quarantine thinking of myself as a writer, but now I do, and I feel so very grateful for that undeniable silver lining. This part of myself clearly existed all along, but to recognize and cultivate it, I needed space and time—two precious gifts the COVID lockdown bestowed in abundance. Elizabeth Gilbert said, "The universe buries strange jewels deep within us all, and then stands back to see if we can find them." Indeed. This is my prayer: In some small way, may reading this book inspire you to go deep, too, to discover some nuggets of treasure inside yourself. They are there. I'm sure of it.

CHAPTER 1

Ample Waves of Gray

The name I've given this opening chapter—my careful wading into the shallows before I plunge into more intimate depths—is a phrase that originally popped into my brain quite suddenly during my morning meditation one day, well over a year ago. It arose in my mind again just recently, resounding within me so powerfully as to influence this entire book, including its title, but when the phrase first showed up in my consciousness, I was simply amused by it. I recognized it as a riff on the line "amber waves of grain" from the song "America the Beautiful" and wondered what it could possibly have to do with me. Over time, I embraced it as an uncanny description not only of myself but also of the actual process of healing, even of life itself. Beyond reflecting the obvious—my hair is gray and wavy—each individual word, as well as the distinct phraseological combination, contains powerful echoes of the journey that I've been privileged to take the last four years.

I say *privileged* because that's the truth of it. Without my husband, Rick, acting as the steadfast keeper of our material realm,

I would not have had the freedom to blaze off on the heroine's journey—a more subtly nuanced, deeply interior process played out in the private sphere of the psyche than the prototypical hero's journey consisting of trials played out in the public realm, though no less earth shattering or life altering for the one taking it or for those around her. For me, it has been an exhilarating, painful, messy, arduous, funny, enlightening journey of recovery from trauma, a vast subterranean movement from mindlessness toward mindfulness, from brokenness toward wholeness, from frozenness toward aliveness. And the timing of my journey was such that, right now, despite experiencing the horrors of our global crisis and being at the advanced age of sixty-one, I strangely find myself so much happier and healthier, so much more engaged and alive than ever before in my life (or than I ever thought possible), which must be why "ample waves of gray" has bubbled back up.

The phrase physically describes me, but perhaps more importantly, metaphorically captures the hard-won sense of self-acceptance I've reached—partly through age but mostly through trauma recovery—and dwell in more solidly with each passing day. Merriam-Webster defines *ample* as "generous or more than adequate in size, scope, or capacity; generously sufficient to satisfy a requirement or need." Thanks to a profound inner transformation, I now know myself to be exactly that—perfectly ample in this life, profoundly okay as I am, a person of inherent worth just by being.

I no longer worry so much about how other people see me or what other people think of me. I have almost completely transformed my previous default patterns of externalizing my value and objectifying myself. For example, I practice showing up unashamed of my gray hair, age spots, wrinkles, scars, or any of the other markers of my many years on this planet. At first this required an unfathomable level of fortitude, given our achingly ageist and shamefully sexist culture, but now it comes more naturally and easily—like everything—through sheer repetition. It's a practice I see lots of women wrestle with, specifically around gray hair, and more obviously than ever thanks to the upheavals of COVID.

Reflected in the media, the population at large, and my own social circles, the pandemic shutdown of nonessential businesses, hair salons among them, is making it nearly impossible for many to keep up the socially sanctioned, almost mandated, hair-dyeing charade. Gray roots have gone viral, and great fun is being poked at the phenomenon and at the women caught up in it. I love a good laugh, but in this case, I'm more inclined toward anger than amusement, because I've read about and personally listened to the deep angst this supposed comic state of affairs has engendered, and I've tuned into the deeper cultural currents at play. Patriarchy is at the root of this issue—a trauma, massive in scale and structural in nature, perpetuated against women for millennia. A trauma I've been working through my whole life, though only with partial awareness during much of it.

My understanding of the issue is colored by my unique hair history because I went gray quite early in life. I don't remember the exact timeline, but gray first started to show up on my head via two distinct streaks, one on either side of my brow, sometime in my late twenties/early thirties and had taken over completely by my late forties. My mother's hair turned early as well, and except for a very brief period during my adolescence, she sported her natural color with élan, so I had a role model to help me make friends with mine. But I didn't always find it easy. For a few years in my late thirties, I succumbed to peer and social pressure and dyed my hair. First, I had auburn highlights put into my brown-going-gray hair, then dark-blonde ones. Finally, after a stylist weighed in that she didn't think I had "the right coloring to pull off gray hair," I had one all-over dye job of that dark-blonde shade. ("I was blonde as a young child," I told myself, "so this is like going back to my natural state." Oh, the depth of self-delusion.)

At the time, the highlights, originally suggested to me as a "fun way to cover the gray," seemed innocent enough to my still rather unconscious self. Since then, however, I have come to see my getting them, not to mention my succumbing to the total dye job, as a reflection of my own collusion with the you-are-not-okay-ness or you-are-not-enough-ness at the base of our cultural messages to women. The day I "went blonde" brought me to a turning point because when I went home and really studied my image in the mirror, instead of seeing the promised "new and improved me," I saw a tormented stranger looking back at me. She was an almost unrecognizable woman with odd-colored hair, her face twisted in a grimace from the pain of her burning scalp and eyes, her nose wrinkled in distaste from the foul odor of chemicals. In the name of "beauty," I had uncharacteristically dropped more money than some people make in a day and spent three precious hours that I couldn't get back, and I was filled with remorse. In that moment, I stopped being willing to hurt myself, or anyone else, to conform to external opinions about my hair.

That decision to embrace my gray paid off, quite literally in time and money as well as metaphorically in the dawning—two decades before I began to consciously heal from trauma—of a sense of my own innate beauty. I began to choose what was beautiful *to me* and to look for it not just in my outward appearance. As actress Salma Hayek asserted, "People often say that 'beauty is in the eye of the beholder,' and I say that the most liberating thing about beauty is realizing that *you* are the beholder. This empowers us to find beauty in places where others have not dared to look, including inside ourselves." The beauty I began to see most clearly in myself was the kind Ruby Dee, American actress, poet, playwright, screenwriter, journalist, and civil rights activist, declared she most wanted, "the hard-to-get kind that comes from within—strength, courage, dignity." My appreciation of this beauty steadily grew over the years alongside a sense of my own power to choose how I show up in the world, cultural values be damned.

It was anger that nudged me into the final fullness of that power and into a more thorough understanding of how cruelly and furtively culture operates to try to constrain it. The anger unexpectedly arose during a mindfulness class I was taking after my conscious journey of awakening had finally begun. Following a lecture, we broke out into small groups for a sharing exercise. Afterward, I was standing around, chatting with three of the women in my group. Seemingly out of nowhere, one of them, who appeared to be around my same age—late fifties to early sixties—said to me, "I love your hair." After I thanked her, she added, "I could never let my hair go gray like that." Used to my gray by now, decades into sporting it and growing comfortable with the oddly increasing occurrences of this kind of compliment, I innocently asked her, "Why?"

When she (chestnut-skinned and brown-nearly-black-eyed) replied, "My stylist told me I don't have the coloring for it," I (pale-skinned and hazel-eyed) gasped at the familiarity of that haunting phrase, rage rising and insight dawning with exquisite clarity. I paused, took a deep breath, regained my equilibrium, and then looked my fellow suffering sister directly in the eye, smiled, and said softly, "Well, of course they did." She stood stock-still for a moment, her facial expression frozen, poised on the brink of anger herself. Then her body visibly softened, a moue playing briefly across her lips, and, as she shook her head, I saw a gleam of understanding light up her eyes. When I added, "I had a stylist tell me that very same thing many years ago," she relaxed completely, chuckling to herself, and asked sardonically, "Just what do you suppose that *right* coloring is?"

Now, tempting as it might be to do so, I don't think that woman's stylist (or the one who said those same pat words to me) was a person of questionable motives, purposely feeding her a line to keep her locked into the endless cycle of dyeing and touch-ups that constitutes the monetary backbone of most hair salons. If only it were that simple. These professionals, and the many others who have parroted that phrase, "You don't have the right coloring for gray hair," are more likely unwitting products of the beauty industrial complex—the enormous web of corporations, large and small, born from men's ideas of what women "should" look like, hell-bent on selling products to enhance what's "right" or fix what's "wrong," happy to profit obscenely off the shame and low self-worth they themselves generate and perpetuate. This is simply one reflection of the deeply entrenched and still-too-widely practiced devaluation and objectification—traumatization—of women in our culture.

Social science characterizes *objectification* as the viewing of another person as an instrument to be used for sexual goals, and in our patriarchal society, women have historically been the objectified ones. But here's the truly insidious part: This objectification is not just perpetrated by men. Many women, collectively over millennia and individually over our own personal lifetimes, have gradually absorbed the warped biases of our ancestors, families, and cultures so well that we self-objectify, without even realizing we're doing it. These biases are baked right into the systems that raise us, rendering them nearly impossible to notice, perhaps more so for women of my generation than those coming after the waves of feminism.

I think about the conditioning I received very early in life to always check in the mirror before leaving the house to make sure I looked just so, and how long I then bound myself to that precept. That learned prioritization of my appearance over my substance, over all the numerous personal characteristics I possessed as a human, set me up so that as I contemplated going out into the world, I regarded myself primarily as a body to be seen. One of my very first memories reflects this focus on appearance—so quickly laid on girl children—and resurfaced chillingly during trauma recovery. In the scene, I'm around three or four years old, sitting outside on the grass and happily amusing myself with a favorite stuffed toy. I'm paying no attention to the several adults encircling me in lawn chairs, sipping cocktails and chatting. That is until one of them—an older man, probably in his sixties, a next-door neighbor—says to my mother, "She's a classic beauty," and I realize with a start that he's staring at and speaking about me.

It was beyond my cognitive abilities at the time to understand how bizarre that statement was, how inappropriate when gazing upon a chubby-cheeked toddler innocently playing, but my body understood—and remembered. To this day, I recall how the back of my neck prickled and my tummy tightened, how I squirmed uncomfortably in the light of his eerie regard. And I know that I'm not the only woman who received that kind of message—subtle or not so subtle, delivered by family or culture—while still very young. Messages repeated over and over as we grew, making it so that whenever we considered ourselves, our first thought was not *Who am I?* but *How do I look?*

Adding another knife twist to that cunning oppression, the "how" we should look has historically been defined very narrowly, in ways that have morphed radically over time as men's preferences have shifted. To flesh out that truth, one need only contrast a Rubens oil painting of a voluptuous nude from the 1600s with a Beaton photograph of skinny Twiggy from the 1960s—to take a relatively recent and strictly Eurocentric perspective. Or look at preferences in the United States, where until all too recently mainstream culture's exalted ideals for women's appearance were unquestionably white, despite the vast diversity of the population. And now, with the advent of digital image manipulation, "beauty standards" have become incongruous for any real flesh-and-blood woman, at any age. Body and appearance shame undergird and undermine women's lives, causing us to revile much about our natural selves, including gray hair.

But why? The answer may have something to do with the perverse fusion of procreation and sexuality in our culture. Maybe the "logic" goes something like this: Women are objects of sexual goals; since sex is for procreation, gray hair (which usually appears after prime childbearing years) means the woman is no longer "valuable"; ergo, gray hair is bad. It's twisted, I know. Or maybe people's discomfort with it has to do with fear of mortality. Gray hair shows up (once again, usually) when we're in our later years, when it becomes increasingly more difficult to ignore that we are indeed getting older, on our way to dying sooner rather than later. Instead of embracing and accepting that undeniable natural fact, our enculturated existential terror has spawned multibillion-dollar industries whose sole function is to deny that fact or at least avert our gaze from it. That's twisted, too, isn't it?

The reasons why women have been conditioned to believe that gray hair is shameful and should be covered could probably fill a book, and I won't spend any more time speculating on them. Instead, let's return to the simple fact that it is just cultural conditioning. It's not cold, hard fact. I see it like diamonds, only in reverse. Diamonds are just rocks, and they command ridiculous prices at the jewelry store only because we humans decided to assign them positive worth. Well, somewhere along the line, we similarly pronounced judgment on gray hair, but this time as a negative—not for men, mind you, just for women. As with all cultural assessments, though, it's up to each of us to decide if it aligns with our own personal ones and to act accordingly. Authenticity is one of my most sacredly held values, and, for me, that definitely doesn't square with hiding my hair.

You might ask, "But what if I just want to dye my hair for fun?" In the spirit of freedom of expression—after all, women should be able to do with their hair as they wish—I'd like to reply, "By all means, go for it!" But I can't say that in good conscience because I struggle to see how dumping chemicals on one's head can possibly serve one's overall health or that of the environment. Women—both personally and collectively—and the planet herself pay a lethally high price to abide by the tenets of the extant beauty industrial complex. If you happen to find some natural, eco-friendly, alternative way to color your hair, all for the good, I suppose. But, even in that case, I implore you, please make sure your use of it is really about fun and not about some sense of inadequacy or some buried fear. Get quiet; search your body, mind, and spirit; find out what your true motives are. Then make your choice.

Choice is the operative word here, and it is key. Habit, compulsion, or reaction, among other unconscious behaviors, can often seem like choice. But, as I have learned through trauma recovery, none of them really are. I now know that at the root of true conscious choice dwells a deep internalized sense of safety, personal power, and freedom, and I have to wonder how many women in our patriarchal culture actually possess that sense. Not because of any personal weakness, but because the deck has been so formidably stacked against us.

Even though the natural wisdom that came with aging lent me a bit of that blessed internal sense, I know I certainly didn't possess it to any great degree until rather recently. I couldn't have, really, given the unresolved traumas of my early years and the fact that I didn't face them until late in life. Nor do I think I'm particularly unique, especially in my generation. When I look at younger folks coming up behind me and the general waking up that seems to be happening, I do feel encouraged for the future, however.

I like to imagine what the impact on the world will be once all women operate from that deep sense of safety, personal power, and freedom 24/7/365. I have a hunch the force of that reality will alter all life, even the planet itself, in profoundly positive ways. I'm convinced that if global leadership had been shared equally with women over the past millennia, human existence would have played out very differently: War wouldn't necessarily be our go-to way for resolving conflict; a more communal approach to raising children would probably dominate instead of the nuclear family model; and institutional and organizational structures would likely echo circular forms not just hierarchical ladders, to name a few of the possible differences that occur to me. Maybe we wouldn't even have had the COVID outbreak. Because I can guarantee you, with reproductive decision-making firmly in female hands, the planet would not have gotten so grossly overpopulated, and we might not have so egregiously encroached on wild land and creatures, which is what brought us into contact with this deadly virus.

But, alas, for far too long humanity denied authority to half of itself, and here we are. For the sake of each and every one of us, for the sake of the earth, we need to continue to transform the oppressive parts of our culture that have led us to our now. Social change always begins with individual choices, maybe even with something as seemingly superficial as whether or not to dye our hair. So, I'm hoping that the opportunity for awakening that has been tragically, but apparently necessarily, provided by this pandemic will lead women to decide to give up the charade, raise the middle finger to the beauty industrial complex, and let their gray shine through in all its glory. I'm hoping they will decide to put the time, energy, and money that would have otherwise gone into covering up a benign truth about their physical being into something that nurtures their inner self, inspires their creativity, broadens their mind, or enlivens their body. In so doing, they will take a step toward healing trauma, for themselves, for all of us, and for the planet.

Before I bring this chapter to a close, I have a confession to make. I might have gone gray with pride relatively early in my life, but patriarchal culture still had a firm hold on me, and I battled appearance shame in other ways. It was many years after I liberated my natural hair color, but before I stopped wearing cosmetics completely, that the significance of the term *makeup* finally hit me. When it did, I asked myself some important questions about why I was putting on foundation or blush or mascara: *Am I making up for supposed flaws? Am I making up a persona?* I didn't like the answers I found within, so not that long ago, I started going barefaced, showing all the world the real me, the naked truth. But, hey, life's a process, and I've tended to take it one transformation at a time. At least until recently, that is, when a constellation of crises occurred, and pretty much everything in my life started to change all at once.

CHAPTER 2

Hitting the Wall

As I peer out at the health crisis sweeping across the entire globe, shutting down everything and everyone in its wake, upending life as we've known it, perhaps even calling our very existence into question, I can't help but recall my own encounter, almost five years past, with crisis. Mythologists Jean Shinoda Bolen, Joseph Campbell, and others assert that all passages of personal transformation (dare we hope planetary as well?) begin with it, but in my case, an entire constellation of crises—three major, two minor—got my heroine's journey rolling. I've variously dubbed what nearly destroyed me as the dark night of the soul, the straw that broke the camel's back, when the shit hit the fan, or the big crash and burn because to get my attention, my poor soul really had to amplify the call. So, let me outline what landed at my door all at once, prompting—no, demanding—my total overhaul.

First, I suffered a head injury in a freak accident. It happened at five-thirty on the chilly dark morning of September 15, 2015, during a U.S. Masters Swimming team workout. I was on a full-bore backstroke sprint for time, arms windmilling rhythmically, legs churning up waves, body rotating smoothly with every pull, head straight, lungs bursting, trying with all I had—I thought—to beat my personal best. Turned out, I wasn't trying with all I had. I had left my mind out of the game, which is a dangerous thing to do. I forgot to pay attention to the bright blue-and-white signal flags stretched across the pool—the ones that let you know you're within a few strokes of the end—and slammed the crown of my head at speed into the unforgiving concrete wall.

On impact, I heard a deafening bang as if an explosive device had detonated inside my skull, saw jagged flashes of bright light behind my eyes, and felt a sickening crunch in my neck. To indicate how out of touch with my body I was at that time, after briefly pulling myself together, I actually tried to continue the workout. Of course, that didn't last. I was too disoriented. When I hauled myself out of the water and explained to the coach why I was leaving early, there was laughter all around, a kind of commiseration between veteran swimmers: "Yup. I've done that before." Even amidst all the publicity about the dangers of concussion that were coming out in the media at that very time—mostly around football—there was no suggestion that I ought to take my injury seriously and seek medical attention. So, I didn't. I also ignored all the growing signs that something was really off and even went to work that day.

However, as I now know, the body will not be denied, and I was quickly forced to pay attention. By not seeking initial care and trying to push through the injury, compounded by factors like my gender, age, and previous history of head injuries, within a few days I had developed a full-blown case of post-concussion syndrome (PCS). This rendered me constantly nauseous and dizzy, unable to concentrate or even think straight, and plagued by intermittent migraines. I had to quit my job, quit life in general, really, to heal. When I wasn't undergoing cranial MRIs or seeing the neurologist, I could be found in one spot: hunkered on the couch for countless hours, waiting for the world to stop spinning, my stomach to cease its turmoil, and my mind to come back online. I wondered if this agonizingly dysfunctional state was my new normal or if I would ever feel well again. This being my third concussion, the answer to those questions was not clear, which added to my suffering.

The PCS eventually subsided completely—a year and a half later—but only ten months after the blow to my head, as I was just beginning to stabilize and actually have hope that I would, over time, regain my previous level of health, the second major crisis hit. According to a witness, an oversized pickup truck going forty-five miles an hour clipped my bicycling husband's back with its extended side mirror, sending him flying over the handlebars. Rick crashed to the ground, slid across the pavement, and crumpled in a heap against the curb. EMTs stabilized him on the scene, then transported him to the nearest trauma center, where I would later find him with eighteen broken bones, a collapsed lung, massive bruising, and head-to-toe road rash, his skull in a cranial stabilizer and various tubes draining bilious colored liquids from his chest and abdomen.

At the time of his accident, I was languorously enjoying a gentle swim at our community center, basking in the progress I was finally starting to make. I'll never forget how quickly my celebratory mood flipped to dread when I got out of the pool, looked at my phone, and saw that during my brief time in the water it had exploded with activity—not the norm for me. There were multiple voice mails from my son, Eric, who almost exclusively texts, and several from a number I didn't recognize. I listened to the messages with mounting alarm, until the last one flooded my veins with ice and stopped me cold. After introducing herself as Charise, an ER nurse, the disembodied voice said, "Your husband is stable now, so I don't want you to worry, but I think it would be a good idea if you came down here as soon as you can. . . ."

When I answered another call from the hospital only a few days later and heard "Mrs. Davidson, this is Debbie from the Rapid Response team," that same feeling of dread returned, but even stronger, such that I had to sit down for fear of passing out. This nurse went on to tell me Rick had developed a sudden-onset internal bleed and was undergoing more emergency procedures to save his life. I felt numb and panicked at the same time, stunned to my core, and had to call a friend to drive me to the hospital so I could be with Rick when—if—he made it out of surgery and into intensive care. Phoning this grim news to Eric—who had only just left San Diego the day before to go home to Tucson, happily assured that his dad was going to survive—took every ounce of energy I had while I waited for my ride.

Thankfully, the trauma team was nothing short of brilliant, and my husband recovered over time. But only a few days after he nearly bled to death, crisis number three presented itself. Rick's beloved uncle and aunt, Hank and Althea, a lively couple well into their eighties and fiercely independent, asked me to come by for a visit for a personal update instead of a phoned-in report on Rick's condition. Even though it meant a fifty-mile round trip, I was more than happy to oblige. Blessed to have them in my life and grateful for our ongoing relationship of mutual love and respect, I would have done anything for them and made a date to stop by the next afternoon. As usual, the door to their apartment swung open at my knock, but my customary sense of happiness upon entering their home veered toward alarm as soon as I took my first step through the door. Grit crunched loudly as my foot hit a filthy floor, and chaotic levels of clutter on every flat surface greeted my gaze.

My heart seized when my eyes lit on Althea and Hank themselves. Always nattily dressed and impeccably groomed, they both appeared uncharacteristically disheveled: hair unkempt, clothing rumpled, even stained. An anguished cry of *No, no, no, not them too. Not now,* resounded in my head. But I pushed past the mounting fear that was fast freezing my insides, rallied momentarily, and kept the visit as light and brief as I could manage. After leaving, I tried to chalk up any seeming disarray to the strain of their nephew's brush with death, and I resolved to pop in more regularly during this trying time. Over the next couple of visits, however, it became clear that their distress went way beyond a reaction to Rick's plight and that they had been struggling for some time and not sharing it with us.

Childless themselves, Rick's uncle and aunt had adopted our little family of three as their own, something my husband, son, and I welcomed. We'd adopted them right back, relishing the many gifts our intergenerational bond had brought over the years. Now, as I gently poked around in their lives, I discovered pressing financial, health, and legal issues that needed to be addressed immediately to ensure their well-being. With Rick out of commission, the responsibility fell to me. So, I began to look after their needs, too, shepherding them to doctor's and lawyer's appointments, wrangling with financial institutions, and arranging for housekeeping help.

With all this intense human drama going on, as declining elders joined wounded husband and recuperating self on my list of people requiring my urgent care, the load already threatening to overwhelm me, the fourth blow struck. My dearly beloved fourteen-year-old dog, Patrick, who had been in gradually declining health for some time, began to fail precipitously. An adorably funny-looking light-tan mutt with a long tail, silky black ears, and a twisted front leg, this rescue had wormed his way into my heart like no other canine I'd ever had before, and he now began to actively die. I found myself adding handfeed-

ing, lifting and moving him when needed, and providing hospice
-like end-of-life care for him on top of visiting Rick in the hospital and tending to Hank and Althea. Self-care rapidly faded
from my activities.

Finally, because I guess every story warrants some dark humor,
a neighbor began regularly posing naked in their front yard. A
fact I discovered quite by accident one morning when heading
out for a walk, shortly after my husband was released from the
hospital to begin the at-home phase of his convalescence. I'm sure
that at another time in my life, under more normal circumstances,
my neighbor's new nudist habit might not have qualified as crisis
number five. It probably wouldn't have bothered me much. Perhaps I would have been able to see it as the cry for help it probably
was, or at least recognize a struggling soul and respond appropriately. But, as you may imagine, at this particular moment, I
didn't have any bandwidth left to handle this person or the neigh-
borhood theatrics that their exhibitionism brought on. Absurdly,
it felt like a big deal, hugely upsetting, while at the same time I
couldn't muster the energy to care. I had nothing left in my tank.

I felt utterly overwhelmed, swamped, barely able to cope. I'm
sure if I had taken the Holmes-Rahe Stress Inventory at that time,
the score would have definitely landed me in the "80 percent
chance of a health breakdown" category—and that's without even
taking into account that the scale allows a full year for the stressful
events to take place, while I endured them almost simultaneously.
I guess it's no wonder that I became quite sick—miraculously not
with a catastrophic illness but dis-eased enough to bring me to my
knees, blow away all my delusions of well-being, and expose the
utter fragility of my defenses in one vivid moment of realization
forever burned in my memory.

I was gazing at myself—my mouth and tongue, specifically—in
the mirror. I hadn't slept but a few hours a night in weeks. Familiar

life-sucking tendrils of anxiety and depression curled around my brain. I struggled with a raging cold that had seemingly taken up permanent residence in my respiratory tract. And now, I had an extremely painful oral thrush infection—something normally only infants and the very old get because their immune systems are so weak. As I stared disbelievingly at the angry scarlet tissues, hugely swollen and covered in hideous white lesions, and felt the throbbing soreness and intense burning that tormented any attempt to swallow or eat, it hit me: *I'm internalizing all this stress.* With laser-like clarity, I understood that I was taking the whole mess of my life out on myself, on my poor body, and that if I kept going this way, I would surely develop major medical problems. I knew in that instant that I absolutely had to change how I dealt with stress. Now, I can cleanly divide my life into before and after this defining moment.

I can't help but wonder, are we—is human history—at a similar defining moment right now? I suspect so. I don't think life will ever return to what it was pre-COVID. Indeed, I don't think that it possibly can, or more importantly, even ought to. I'm convinced that returning to living as I had been before my crucible of crises would have led to my downfall, hastened my death. My approach was unsustainable—as is how we are currently inhabiting this planet and relating to one another—and called for radical change. Somehow, I found the strength to make the needed changes, changes that have in turn helped me navigate this time of world crisis from a stronger, more resilient place. I hope and pray that together we can find a way to make similar shifts in the collective. As I discovered after my defining moment, the first order of business is to get real.

CHAPTER 3

Riding Waves with Mindfulness

Before my defining moment in 2016, if you'd asked me if I was happy with life in my late fifties, I'm sure I would have said yes. I had interesting work, a nice home, a caring family, decent health, and my sanity. All appeared well on the outside. With the benefit of hindsight and hard-earned greater personal awareness, however, I've peered more closely at my life back then and seen the cracks in the facade, the depth of pain I carried around inside while smiling for the world. At the time, I might have flippantly said, "Sure, I have some problems, but who doesn't?" But I secretly led that all too ubiquitous "life of quiet desperation" famously described by Thoreau. I was not being real.

Yes, I mostly enjoyed my job, but every damn day as I drove up the long, winding driveway to the office, a feeling of dread would grow in the pit of my stomach. To quell it, I'd have to repeat to myself, *You can do this. It's only six hours.* Yes, I lived in a comfortable house in one of the indisputably loveliest cities in the United States, but I didn't really feel at home where I found myself and often wished I were somewhere else. Yes, I loved my husband and

my son, and they loved me, but a sense of missing important relational depths with both of them gnawed at me constantly. Yes, I
could claim generally good physical health, but I struggled with
intermittent insomnia, almost chronic constipation, and a myriad
of musculoskeletal symptoms that too frequently curbed my natural penchant for activity, sometimes for months on end. Yes, I
successfully managed lifelong emotional symptoms diagnosed earlier in my life as bipolar II, but I hated to my core that I ingested
psychoactive medications daily to accomplish that stability. All
was not well.

Thanks to getting real, however, I can happily report—four-
plus years after my defining moment—that every one of those
struggles (and more) has been transformed. As for quiet desperation, I now mostly live out loud, and I recognize any hopelessness,
which only rarely arises anymore, as a welcome arrow pointing me
back to an old wound in need of my attention. I no longer take
medication, having learned that my troubling emotional symptoms were about unresolved trauma—not an inherent chemical
imbalance—and undertaken the work to recover from it. (Important note: like the small print in TV ads, I must caution, "Please do
not try this at home." My weaning off meds and the concurrent
healing process have been long, slow, careful, and fully supported
by brilliant professionals. More on this later.)

I've befriended my body, prioritized its care, and now enjoy not
simply good but vibrant health. The symptoms that used to plague
me are gone such that, on an almost constant basis, I'm blessed with
regular and easeful sleep and elimination and the absence of joint or
muscle aches and pains. I feel strong and flexible, and I'm filled with
energy and vitality. I can now not only swim, walk, and hike as regularly as I like, but also take to the floor for hours in my conscious
dance community (albeit online at this COVID moment) with the
same esprit and stamina as people half my age. Most importantly,

I've learned to hear and heed my body's messages more quickly and to work with energy and movement for healing when issues first appear, which I'll also explore later in this book.

I've discovered the power of conscious presence and vulnerability in relationship so I show up very differently in my marriage and as a mother. I now enjoy deeper, more honest, and more mutually supportive bonds with my husband of twenty-eight years and with my twenty-six-year-old son than I ever thought possible. I've woken up to the moment, looked around, and realized that I'm absolutely where I am meant to be, and always have been, every step of the way. I feel enormous gratitude that I get to live where I do and have a home that shelters me, and I no longer pine to be anywhere else. Finally, I have vocations I love thoroughly and completely: my writing and dancing. Each day, I eagerly sit at the computer and play with words, or I get down with the music and the rhythms, often both.

How did this epic transformation happen? What did "getting real" look like? For me, the first step was mindfulness. I'm aware this word crops up everywhere these days, and some folks are tired of hearing it. Catapulted from fringe to mainstream in the last couple of decades, it's grown into a buzzword (arguably detrimentally so, as even soulless corporations now attempt to wield it as a tool to increase productivity and shareholder profits). But without it, quite honestly, I might not even be alive. In the maelstrom of stress I experienced a few years back, I was most assuredly on a crash course with major illness, but blessedly, following my defining moment in front of the mirror, the word *mindfulness* popped into my brain unbidden.

I had dabbled in it before, but rather unfruitfully, declaring to anyone who would listen, "I just can't do mindfulness. My brain won't shut off." Of course, I'd gotten it all wrong, since mindfulness isn't about clearing one's mind, but rather paying attention to it. Thankfully, I stopped heeding my own well-rehearsed line. Instead, I just sat down at the computer, googled "mindfulness in San Diego," and there it was—my lifeline. UC San Diego's Center for Mindfulness was offering an eight-week Mindfulness-Based Stress Reduction (MBSR) program. Bingo! Stress? I had it in spades. Reduction? I needed it desperately. I registered on the spot, sensing that it was a matter of life and death (if not literal death, at least a kind of living death).

I rejoice that I listened to that still, small voice whispering inside me, because taking that MBSR course laid the solid foundation for what would grow into a yearslong healing journey of profound and permanent change. I didn't foresee the trajectory at the time of registration, nor did I suspect it on my first day of class when I walked into that peaceful, window-lined gathering room looking out onto the lush, leafy courtyard. I thought I was in this gig for eight short weeks, that life would get fixed, and I'd be on my merry way. But I was in for a host of surprises, the first of which was that, through MBSR, I'd begin the exploration of my mind by getting up close and personal with my body. Something I'd never really done before.

The first formal practice MBSR teaches, and assigns for daily homework, is a forty-five-minute guided meditation that invites participants to pay attention to their body, slowly and deliberately, part by part, starting with the toes of one foot and winding up at the face and head. On the surface, this may seem like a mundane, even easy, exercise, but it can be quite challenging. Sometimes when the guide had us focus, say, on the ankle, I'd tune out, only to come back to myself and find we were now already at the chest. Or I'd get to my knee, feel pain, and freak out, then mentally ruminate over its imagined doomsday significance and lose the train completely. Or sometimes I'd just feel nothing—no sensation at all—for long periods of the meditation.

But slowly, with daily repetition, I began to access and sustain contact with my body for longer and longer periods of time, sensing into the tingling in my toes, the throbbing at my calf, the gurgling in my belly, the ache in my chest, the beat of my heart, the lump in my throat, the buzzing in my head—whatever I found—without condemning, running away, catastrophizing. Without reacting. I've heard musicians speak eloquently of becoming one with their instrument through the discipline of practice, which describes my shift exactly. Through practice, I went from experiencing my body—my instrument—as something outside myself, almost like an enemy constantly letting me down with its various aches or dysfunctions, to knowing it *as* me, my own most trusted friend, a font of information, a source of wisdom I could ask, "What are you trying to tell me with this sensation?"

Starting with the body scan and progressing through the many other practices and wealth of information MBSR offered, I learned how to, as John Kabat-Zinn, developer of the program, put it, "pay attention, in the present moment, on purpose and without judgment" to my inner and outer experience. I became aware of how much my mind focused on the past or the future instead of the now, and how much old unconscious patterns drove me and shaped my interactions and life. I developed tools and skills to shift my awareness to current reality and establish new habits of behavior that serve me more healthfully. I'm still very much a work-in-progress and will be, gloriously, for the rest of my life. But I've practiced the learnings—in one manner or another, formally and informally—every day (almost without exception) since I began MBSR, and I live so differently now; it's like night and day, before and after.

In MBSR, I found learning about the nuts and bolts of brain function and conditioning, the biology of stress and reactivity, and our negativity bias and default mode network enormously helpful. All of it normalized so much about my past. I also found it hugely exciting to discover that by using the practices of MBSR I could literally rewire my own brain, which gave me tremendous hope for my future. (Thank you, Universe, for the miracle of neuroplasticity.) I'm a bit of a nerd, so this "sciencey stuff" fascinated me, fed my intellectual self. Unexpectedly, though, the course also reawakened my spiritual side.

I guess that shouldn't have surprised me, really, since MBSR is secularly derived, in part, from ancient Buddhist teachings that honor the essential integration of body, mind, and spirit. A fact Western science is bumping up against, thousands of years later. Both perspectives are starting to agree that human beings cannot be partitioned into physical, mental, and emotional segments to be treated separately. Humans must be viewed and healed in a more integrative fashion, as complex multidimensional systems, wholes to be reckoned with that are greater even than the sum of their parts. That idea resonates strongly with me when I remember I was the poster child for how reductionist thinking doesn't work, as evidenced by my deep angst about, and devastating side effects from, the "triumph" of pharmacologically managed moods. Not to mention a life that still wasn't working terribly well despite chemical intervention.

It's working well now, though, most notably with a sense of equanimity that bolsters me with its abiding presence, a deep calm steadiness I've felt particularly grateful for during this topsy-turvy pandemic. All those hours spent tuning in to my body and mind, all that "time on the cushion," as mindfulness practice is affectionately called, made a huge difference in my life. (Note: sitting cross-legged on a meditation cushion is not required; lying on the floor or sitting in a chair for body scan or meditation do me just fine, thank you.) I would describe the most salient feature of that difference as a sense of space—room to pause, witness my experience, and choose a response, instead of immediately reacting to external stimuli or internal cues. A sense that has helped me negotiate the near-constant barrage of chaos in the world at this moment in time. That's the whole point of practice. Not to achieve some transcendent state, above it all, but to live more skillfully and healthfully, right here, on the ground, in the day-to-day. I'm so grateful that my plunge into mindfulness came before the tsunami of COVID hit.

I still feel all there is to feel as a human, including those emotions we are wont to label negative such as sadness, anger, or fear. But now, because of the path MBSR started me down, I can greet them, embrace them, and trust in them as guides, à la Rumi's poem "The Guest House." By not averting from any emotions, or clinging to them, I get to watch them wash through me like waves. And it's not just emotions I've learned to welcome, it's my thoughts, images, states, and sensations—every phenomenon of my life. They all arise, dwell for a bit, and then pass on. (As do all phenomena in the world. It's Nature's way.)

Just as when ocean waves recede and leave behind smooth sand, I've found that these various waves of my life force clear the way to inner wisdom and insight. When they ebb, I understand where I need to go next on my healing journey, and I find my way there organically. And just like receding surf uncovers beautiful shells or other treasure, on the other side of the swells of fear, anger, and sadness, I've found the gift of joy. Before mindfulness, I don't think I ever felt real joy, but for once or twice in my life. And I suspect this is because the amplitude of waves matter.

When I relied on medication, my life force was flattened (but not in a life-saving way like we're trying to do with lockdown in the face of the coronavirus). Then, I could ride up and down a little crest of sadness, and maybe I'd come out into happiness. Now, free of all artificial alteration, I can ride a big billow of, say, grief, and when I do, I release into joy—deep, abiding joy. As with equanimity, joy also sustains my life now. Because I've gone to the depths, faced and fully felt in an embodied and supported way the most difficult aspects of my life, I've surfaced into the realm of bliss. I don't live there continuously—I'm fully human after all, perfectly imperfect, if you will. But I know that joy will always return. It is my birthright.

I've gotten ahead of myself here, because it wasn't just one eight-week class that enabled my joyful surfing of the waves of life. I don't want you to get the impression that I entered MBSR a mess, and *poof*, eight weeks later I dwelled in nirvana. Far from it. While the course did get the process started, other modalities, tools, and people played vital roles during my epic odyssey to well-being. Soon after MBSR, however, my healing journey really took off, and just like mindfulness beginning with the body, the acceleration started in an unexpected place.

CHAPTER 4

Compassion Saved Me

Maybe I had my head in the sand, but I'd not much heard the word *compassion* until I started MBSR in 2017. When the class instructors first introduced the concept—empathetic consciousness of suffering coupled with the desire to alleviate it—it felt cumbersome and archaic to me, and I doubted that it would help me deal with stress. However, I soon repented my sorely misplaced skepticism. For me, compassion is fundamentally the heart of the matter. Let me explain how I gained that understanding, and why I audaciously claim that compassion saved me.

As I began to learn how to pay attention to my thoughts, feelings, and sensations, I noticed some patterns emerge. The most striking of these—because of its frequency and aggressiveness—I started calling my judgmental mind. Even before practicing mindfulness, I had bumped up against the awareness that I adopted an overcritical attitude at times. I grew up in a family that, over generations, had perfected the fine art of pronouncing swift and almost exclusively negative sentences upon others based on trivial details like clothing or on deeper issues like religion. I had simmered in that narrow-minded soup during my formative years, but I'd also worked as an adult, somewhat successfully I had thought, to put aside summary judgment. Apparently not.

During MBSR, I came face-to-face with how much of a knee-jerk reaction judgment was for me: it was my go-to, my most insidious automatic-pilot setting. To use a mundane example, when someone cut me off in traffic, I noticed that the words *What a jerk* would immediately pop into my mind—in a split second. What really got my attention about this unconsciously critical pattern was when I discovered that it caused *me* to suffer unnecessarily. My own instantaneous negative verdict initiated a powerful cascade of stress in my body. An event or interaction didn't cause me pain as much as my reaction to it did. That realization rose starkly when I started to use a brilliant awareness practice, taught in MBSR and aptly named STOP (Stop. Take a breath. Observe. Proceed.).

Going back to that car in traffic, I found that if I could pause just long enough to take a breath and halt my automatic judgment, my elevated heart rate and shallow breathing (natural sympathetic nervous system responses to a close call on the highway) returned to normal very quickly. When I failed to maintain present moment awareness and allowed that old hardwired negative thought pattern to activate, my heightened state continued much longer, even grew in intensity. I'd get swept up in what an asshole that person was, what a terrible thing they had done to me, how it could've caused a horrible accident, and on and on. My own thoughts fueled my aggravation.

This same ironic realization seemed to dawn on almost everyone in my MBSR class. We had all come to the course because something in our lives was not going well—relationships, work, health, finances, you name it—and, for the most part, we each understood that *we* needed to change for our lives to go more smoothly. We came in accepting responsibility. However, I'm not sure any of us anticipated the extent to which MBSR would keep pointing us back to ourselves, to our very own habits of mind, as the cause of our most acute suffering. I'm reminded of a phrase from Walt Kelly's *Pogo* comic strip: "We have met the enemy, and he is us."

Part of the effectiveness, the brilliance, of MBSR is that it takes place in a group where participants are invited to share their process, reflections, insights, challenges, and learnings. I don't remember exactly how many people were in my course, maybe around fifteen to twenty, but I vividly recall the powerful support I felt as we all grappled with the unavoidable truth of personal responsibility. We shared other struggles too. Even though all our main issues were different—a marriage on the rocks, an autoimmune disease, a business bankruptcy, the death of a child—whenever any of us shared a reflection on the impact of the course material or an exercise, several heads around the circle would always nod in silent recognition.

Sensing all this similarity, I began to feel less alone in my challenges and found an odd comfort in the reality of others' troubles, experiencing this as a warmth suffusing my body, a quieting of my churning mind, and a buoyancy in my spirit. The actual felt sense of compassion had dawned inside of me. I had taken in—with my whole being—the core concept of common humanity, and I now understood, in a deep internal way, that while each being may be unique, reflecting our blessed diversity, we do share some experiences, thoughts, emotions, and sensations universal to *Homo sapiens*. I'd embodied the truth that we're all in this together.

What really clinched the compassion thing for me, though, was an exercise we did that dove into the idea of the "stories in our heads." One of the teachers asked us to settle in our seats, close our eyes, take a few deep breaths, and picture ourselves walking down a sidewalk where we lived, encouraging us to imagine as many details as possible so that we really began to sense into the scene and feel the experience. Next, she had us picture a friend of ours coming toward us from the other direction, ourselves greeting them, and that person passing us by without saying anything. After bringing us out of this visualization, she invited us to share what had first popped into our minds and hearts when our greeting went unacknowledged.

As you can probably imagine, people responded in a variety of ways. Shame at being ignored arose for some, as did fear of having offended, anger over a perceived snub, and more. In microseconds, every single one of our brains had made up some story to explain what had happened—all based on old unconscious programming because we couldn't possibly know the actual explanation for our friend's behavior. There was none. This was make-believe. I quickly recognized how much this harmful mindless modus operandi of story making was part of my repertoire, and I vowed to try and drop it.

The next time someone cut me off in traffic (yes, this is an astonishingly regular occurrence on Southern California highways) when I wasn't present enough to stop the automatic *What a jerk* reaction, I had another mindfulness tool at my disposal to halt the stress cascade. This time when I noticed my reaction, I asked myself, *Okay, Laurie, why that particular assessment?* I quickly remembered that I truly didn't—couldn't—know the arc of that driver's life in that moment. Maybe they were desperately trying to get a sick child to the hospital or something similarly urgent. That's as equally plausible as their being a jerk, among countless other explanations. Besides, I reflected, in my almost fifty years of driving hadn't I most assuredly cut people off in traffic? Did that make me a jerk?

I could not examine my own ingrained reaction pattern of judgment, see the naked and painful truth of self-condemnation under it, and not feel a communion and connection with the other. I came to understand that compassion wasn't a curricular add-on; it was the natural outgrowth of mindful awareness. Because I was learning to see and be with my own foibles and struggles in a loving and accepting way, I could see them and be with them in others in that very same manner, understanding that while individual circumstances may vary—even radically so—at some fundamental level, we are all united in the challenge of this human existence. Life is hard, it often hurts, and we're each doing the best we can in the moment, even when we cause harm to ourselves or others. Compassion doesn't excuse bad behavior, but it sees beneath it to the pain and wounding that is always at the root of that behavior.

Thankfully, pain is not the full story of human existence. Joy also shines brightly. In fact, studying mindfulness introduced me to the concept of sympathetic joy, a cousin of compassion, in which one consciously shares in another's elation, good fortune, or triumph. However, bear with me while I stick with struggle a little longer, because I'm afraid that at this point in my journey I still had a distance to go before I broke through into the light in a major way.

It's true that MBSR had already helped me shift some big things in my life. Meditating every day, I had begun to feel calmer and stronger. I had changed the way I responded to stressors in my life. I had begun a self-study of neuroscience that was transforming the way I understood what had been previously called my "mental health issues." I now possessed a great deal of new and helpful information and had learned a variety of skillful habits and useful tools to increase my well-being.

I had also learned, though, that I was incredibly cruel to myself—deeply, horrifyingly cruel. Remember my judgmental mind pattern? Well, guess whom it most frequently victimized and at whom it spewed the most vitriol—me. By paying careful attention to my thoughts and feelings, I discovered that I routinely and vehemently said unkind things to myself, things I would never say directly to another human being, not even to someone I didn't like, things that when I think about them even now make me feel like weeping. The actual words themselves didn't gut me as much as the ugly messages lurking underneath them—*you are not okay, you are too much, you are unlovable*—and the deeply painful feelings those messages evoked. For example, when I felt sadness arise one day as I fondly recollected my deceased dog Patrick, I heard a voice in my head shout, *What is wrong with you? That was more than a year ago. Get over it, for God's sake!* Would I have uttered those harsh words to a dear friend who had shared her sadness with me? Absolutely not. I wouldn't even have thought them.

It wasn't easy to face this reality of mind and heart, to reckon with the fact that I'd probably been feeding myself—without noticing—a steadily abusive verbal diet for much of my lifetime, but I did. In the MBSR mid-course evaluation, I wrote that I had gotten in touch with self-cruelty, that I could see that I needed to transform it, and that I planned to sign up to take the UCSD course entitled Mindful Self-Compassion (MSC) next. I remember my teacher's encouraging response: "Good for you. One starts next month." Facing up to something and tackling it are two different things, however, and a full eight months passed before I began MSC. I don't remember why it took me so long to get around to it. I have vague recollections of calendar conflicts, travel plans, and outside commitments getting in the way, but it's probably more accurate to say that I just wasn't ready yet to unpack and heal something so big, so fundamental, so at the core of my being.

Retrospect has helped me see that those eight months constituted an important period of growth and integration that prepared me for the major work to come. I'm not sure I would have had the breakthroughs I've had without them, without the time spent practicing mindfulness, exploring resources, opening to change, and trying on new ways of being—in short, getting ready. I'm reminded of the quote often attributed to Lao Tzu: "When the student is ready, the teacher will appear." And appear it did in the form of a nine-week online MSC course offered through the Center for Mindful Self-Compassion, which I began in January of 2018. I had hesitations about taking something this personal and weighty online (hesitations I now find funny, given how, under the shadow of a virus, much of my life has artfully moved into the digital realm), but I couldn't locate an in-person option that worked with my schedule. I needn't have worried. The MSC course was beautifully done—in a safe and tender manner—and was exactly what I needed.

Together with twenty-odd people from all over the world, I began to learn the fine art of treating myself well. MSC, the brainchild of Kristin Neff and Christopher Germer, equally grounded in the wisdom of ancient Buddhist teachings, the findings of contemporary neuroscience, the insights of clinical practice, and the results of rigorous academic research, is pure genius. As I progressed through the wealth of helpful information and simple yet profound practices, I noticed a positive difference, starting almost immediately, in the tenor of my self-dialogue and accompanying feeling states. Now, if sadness came up, instead of condemning myself for it, I would simply name it: *Sadness is here.* Then I would offer myself some sympathetic words, *I'm sorry you feel sad*, and remind myself of the shared human experience, *Everyone feels this way sometimes.* Finally, after inquiring of myself, *What do you need right now?* I'd follow through with the comforting gesture, or cup of tea, or phone call to a friend that was the answer to that kind question.

This new way of being with myself made any pain or suffering that might arise in my daily life—mental, emotional, physical, or spiritual—feel less acute and allowed it to subside much more quickly in the light of my loving attention. I began to realize, even more than I had through MBSR, that I am never alone because *I* can be here for myself. I had to laugh out loud in joy on the day when my judgmental mind pattern arose to criticize me, and I greeted it with compassion, *I see you, old friend. Thanks for stopping by, but I'm going to think something different.* I said this phrase with my hands placed gently over my heart. Of the many powerfully healing gestures of self-touch MSC had introduced me to, that was the one I had adopted for my own because it brought me almost immediate solace, flooding my body, as tender touch can, with oxytocin. It had become an ingrained habit of care.

MSC ushered in a radical shift in my perspective on where kindness begins—with myself—and I gleefully rode the wave of increased benevolence and happiness that seemed to infuse my life and my relationships the more I practiced self-compassion. That is until I came face-to-face with the phenomenon of backdraft. As the teacher and the course materials both explained, kindness flowing into a newly opened heart (sometimes for the first time ever) can ignite the flames of old buried pain, just like breaking a window or opening a closed door can trigger an explosion or dramatic upsurge in an actual fire that has been oxygen starved. They assured us that MSC backdraft was real and would most likely occur, and they gave us numerous suggestions for tending to ourselves when it did.

My backdraft moment came one day in class during a guided meditation practice. I don't recall the content of the meditation itself, but what I will never forget was how a long-buried memory from childhood arose spontaneously, immediately engulfing me in overwhelming shame. A brief but vivid snippet—me, very young, kneeling on the carpeted floor of my bedroom in confusion and abjection, looking up at my red-faced mother vehemently con-demning me—filled my mind. My reaction was instantaneous and searing: my whole body burned, my chin dropped to my chest, my cheeks flushed, my breath caught, and I absolutely wanted to curl up and disappear, forever. As we had been encouraged to do from the start of the course, I responded in that moment with self-compassion. I pulled out of the meditation, opened my eyes, rose from my chair, and walked around my room, hugging myself, breathing deeply, speaking soothingly, naming my present reality, *Ah, this is backdraft, and old shame is here*, and *Right now, in this moment, I am okay*, until my equilibrium returned.

Like every other human, I had felt shame before. Starting in my twenties, when I first examined having grown up in the shame-based system that is an alcoholic family, and continuing throughout my adult life, I'd reckoned hard with how much shame abided at the core of me—a legacy of that early upbringing. But I'd never felt it so overwhelmingly before, at least not consciously so. I knew right away that I would need additional support to tend to the wounding that must underlie this utterly engulfing experience of it. While I continued with the MSC course, I heeded the final item in their long list of ways to deal with backdraft: "If you need further assistance, please make use of your personal contacts (friends, family, therapists, teachers) to get what you need."

That same day, I reached out to one of the teachers I'd had in MBSR, a psychotherapist who I knew also taught MSC and would be familiar with what I was going through. She was unable to take on a new client at that time, but she enthusiastically referred me to one of her colleagues, Livia Walsh, whose name I immediately recognized. Of all the recorded guided meditations the UCSD Center for Mindfulness provides on their website as resources, Livia's were my favorites because of her soothing vocal timbre, calm pacing, and lovely Boston accent that reminded me of a dear friend. And because she just seemed so very comfortable traversing all parts of the human physical terrain. Over the course of my journey, I had listened to her body scan at least fifty times. I'd never met her, but I felt like I knew her already through that experience, which made calling her and beginning therapy almost easy.

It was no accident that Livia became my therapist. As my journey unfolded, a recurring pattern of my opening to pain and then receiving the exact balm I needed from the Universe was becoming obvious to me and something I could trust. Originally, through her recorded guidance, Livia had unknowingly helped me begin to reinhabit my body. Now, she would purposefully help me go deeper into that process through compassion-based therapy, informed by her own rich contemplative life, extensive nursing background, long years teaching MBSR and MSC, and deep understanding of neuroscience. Livia and I journeyed together for only three months, the shortest amount of time I'd ever engaged with a therapist—and I'd engaged with many over the course of my tumultuous life—but it was life changing.

She helped me make sense of my backdraft moment, to understand its appearance—which had frightened me at the time—as a welcome sign that I had cracked open and was ready to do some important healing work. Even though I told Livia the same stories I'd told previous therapists, she was the first practitioner to recognize and name my generalized sense of unsafety, use the words *abuse* and *trauma* to describe my early experiences, and suggest that they were all physically lodged in my system. With her deeply compassionate awareness of both my needs and her own limitations, Livia warmly and decisively loved, stabilized, informed, and readied me to engage with a more body-based trauma-specific therapy.

All the while, she helped bolster my own budding self-compassion skills, skills that would prove essential for surviving what was to come, for tending kindly to myself as I plumbed as-yet-unimaginable reservoirs of pain. Without this strengthening, I simply would not have been ready for the hard work ahead. The other, and much less widely quoted, half of that Lao Tzu wisdom saying I shared earlier feels so appropriate here: "When the student is truly ready, the teacher disappears." Livia's final act was to guide me right out her door and into the therapeutic realm through which I have come to experience a radical rebirth. So, as you can see, I owe it all—my second chance at life—to compassion. I really do.

CHAPTER 5

⌒ᔕ

Life's a Jigsaw Puzzle

A dear friend of mine is an avid jigsaw puzzler. I've done only a few in my lifetime, not being particularly drawn to them myself; however, listening to her describe her experience, I've been struck by the inspired nature of the jigsaw puzzle. Doing them seems to be a kind of mindfulness discipline, an experience of flow. They also represent an uncanny metaphor for life: Over time, we put the pieces of our lives together as best we can. Sometimes we get stuck; other times, things fall into place easily. Occasionally we see a pattern; often, it all seems random. Perhaps we try to force things together that don't actually fit or we miss the obvious, then by chance, things might click together unexpectedly. We encounter fun and frustration, challenge and triumph, and if we persist, the picture coalesces and great beauty is revealed. I can see why there has been a run on them during the COVID quarantine.

I'm musing on this idea because I find myself hesitating to go right on and tell you about my experience with somatic trauma therapy, even though that's where the story was obviously heading by the end of the last chapter. When my friend showed me how she'll sometimes work on assembling specific sections of a puzzle off to the side, I saw how her process reflected my own life and understood that for you, the reader, to get the entire picture, I needed to take you on a short detour to visit a couple of side sections before going back to the main body of my puzzle. While the central thrust of my journey cut from mindfulness to compassion to somatic therapy—from becoming aware of, to embracing, to transforming trauma—I was also simultaneously exploring other ideas that were key to how it all came together in the end.

In a synchrony too remarkable for me to dismiss as anything other than the benevolent hand of the Universe, toward the end of my three months of compassion-based therapy, the multimedia publishing company Sounds True held a free, ten-day, twenty-four-presenter, live online program entitled The Healing Trauma Summit. At the exact moment that Livia pointed to the reality of trauma in my life, this summit laid out a smorgasbord of the greatest minds in the field, presenting the latest perspectives, understandings, and treatments. I dined at that buffet as much as possible, devouring what my available time allowed. I purposely chose presenters from a wide variety of backgrounds who shared valuable information and practices from contemporary sciences and therapies as well as from ancient wisdom traditions, and whose material focused not just on the personal but also on familial, cultural, and historical trauma and their broader implications for our world.

With each presentation, I felt my mind and heart blow wider and wider open, and my perspective on life begin to shift radically. Perhaps most pertinent to the trajectory of my story is that I first encountered Peter Levine and his Somatic Experiencing (SE) therapy during this summit. Something resonated deep within me as I viewed his presentation, and when I brought it up in my work with Livia, I found she was quite familiar with Peter and his work, specifically with his program for healing sexual trauma—a big part of what she and I had discovered I was facing. I considered the idea of doing his program in audio format on my own, but, together with Livia, decided that a specifically trained flesh-and-blood companion would serve me best in an exploration sure to be deep and raw. That would be my next step.

Another puzzle side section I was working on during this time was an exploration of Somatic Self-Compassion (SSC), a modality developed by Kristy Arbon. I first encountered Kristy during MSC, as an audio of her guided compassionate body scan was one of the resources provided in the course. I fell in love with the Aussie lilt of her voice and her deeply soulful style of guiding meditations. So, once MSC was over and I had some stability through my work with Livia, I decided to explore her website and discovered a treasure trove.

Intrigued by Kristy's specific focus on the body, I signed up to take her online course. Through it, I encountered topics directly related to my experience, which I never would have come across on my own, along with artfully synthesized material from a wide variety of fields like mindfulness and compassion, somatics, trauma, human development, neuroscience, psychology, and more. Studying with her in a group expanded my mind, helped me make important connections in my growing self-understanding, and provided aha moments almost too numerous to count, the biggest being when she delved into Stephen Porges's polyvagal theory.

I'd first encountered the theory, which is revolutionizing the fields of trauma recovery, psychiatry, medicine, nursing, body-work, disaster relief, education, parenting, and others, during the Sounds True summit. Now, with Kristy's assistance, I began to grasp more fully the undeniably physiological nature of trauma that the theory points to. Trauma is not all in our head, as I'd believed for far too long. I won't try to explain the whole theory here because I'd do a terrible job and there are plenty of resources that do it brilliantly. I will say the theory compellingly illuminates the pivotal role of the vagus nerve (which runs from the brain through the heart, lungs, digestive tract, and other organs) in the biology of response to overwhelm. I found the theory a game changer.

It gathered varied aggravating symptoms that I'd contended with my entire life, which had seemed completely unrelated—insomnia, constipation, emotional instability—and united them with a single stroke. Suddenly, they all made sense. I understood that they were simply integral manifestations of my body's systemic response to perceived danger and did not require, in fact would not lastingly benefit from, individual attention. As I see it, the promise of the theory is this: heal the system, and you'll heal the parts. I'm living proof that the promise is real.

Through holistic somatic therapy—grounded in polyvagal theory—I've worked on my whole system, and my previously lifelong symptoms have essentially disappeared. They each might visit briefly from time to time, but they no longer chronically afflict me. If they do show up—those instances are growing farther apart with continued healing—I know I need to look at what's invoking my trauma response and tend to that, not go to the doctor or take a pill. The implications of this understanding are huge, and I'm fascinated by the studies that are finding significant links between trauma and diverse conditions like irritable bowel syndrome, anxiety, asthma, autoimmune disorders, fibromyalgia, attention deficit hyperactivity disorder, depression, and even Alzheimer's and dementia. It gives me great hope for new, better, more holistic paths to well-being.

But I'm getting ahead of myself. Back then, I was just beginning to understand the theory and its implications for my health when Kristy also introduced me to ACEs, and I had another important aha moment. ACE stands for "adverse childhood experience" and comes from a landmark 1990s CDC–Kaiser Permanente study that proved how negative life events occurring before age eighteen—including all types of abuse and neglect as well as parental mental illness, substance abuse, divorce, incarceration, and domestic violence—significantly impact a child's development and lead directly to negative outcomes in adulthood, including mental and physical health problems, substance abuse, and risky behaviors. Again, I heard my experience echoed on a colossal scale and began to think differently about the causes of my past perpetual struggles.

At this same time, Kristy introduced me to attachment theory and its focus on the bond between an infant and their primary caregiver. The theory posits that to grow into an emotionally healthy and resilient adult, an infant needs an emotionally healthy caregiver to securely attach to; otherwise, dysfunctional attachment patterns form that negatively affect the child's behavioral and emotional development right into adulthood. It was easy for me to see how the truth of this dynamic had played out in the turbulent decades of my own life because of the various incapacities of my parents when I was born, especially my poor mother. It wasn't a big leap to understand how my parents themselves had been similarly impacted by their caregivers, who were even less well equipped to provide appropriate nurturance, and on back through our family history.

This understanding helped me see that there are different types of trauma, with distinct imprints. Previously, I had associated the word only with an actual event or events, say an incident of child abuse, a car accident, the premature death of a parent, or an assault. Now I saw that, yes, there's that. It's called acute trauma. And there's also a subtler, almost silent, kind called developmental or attachment trauma. It's formed in the face of an infant's or young child's fundamental needs for feeling safe, seen, heard, and wanted. These basic requirements are not just nice ideas. They are undeniable needs. Numerous studies on mammals have proven that harmful patterns are laid down in their biological, neuro-logical, and energetic systems when these needs are not fulfilled. For humans, findings show that those patterns can include deep-seated unconscious feelings of unsafety, invisibility, unworthiness, and unlovability—a kind of core shame—and lead to profoundly negative life outcomes.

I didn't have to look at studies for proof of this early hard-wiring into the brain and how it carries into adulthood. I just needed to look at myself, at my struggle with self-cruelty. I could see now that this pattern hadn't appeared out of thin air. I'd developed a fierce inner critic as a survival mechanism. As an infant and young child, being utterly dependent on others for survival and with a brain still years away from the capacity for rational thought, the only "conclusion" I could possibly make in the face of repeatedly unmet emotional needs was that there was something wrong with *me*.

I have an early memory illustrative of this phenomenon. It's not a conscious memory, per se, rather a recollection passed on to me by my beloved sister, Leslie, who is five years older than I. Years ago, she told me that she remembers me as a very active, energetic little girl whose vibrancy seemed to overwhelm my parents right from the start. Specifically, Leslie recounted that on more than one occasion, she watched my mother take whatever useful object was at hand and soak it in her martini, then give it to me to suck on, apparently so I would settle down and become more docile and easier to contain. I have a photograph that was taken on one such occasion. I'm about two years old, restrained in a chair, clutching a wet clamshell in my pudgy fist, glassy eyes staring dully at the camera, suitably anesthetized.

At the time, my toddler brain was physically unable to reason out that my poor, stressed, oppressed, depressed mother had done something dreadfully wrong in giving me alcohol to deal with her own discomfort—an understanding I'm perfectly capable of coming to now. Instead, still necessarily and rightfully in survival mode, I concluded: *My energy is too much; I am bad.* Repeated enough times, this kind of experience laid down a well-worn groove, and I learned to keep myself bottled up, in line, "acceptable." It was a brilliant strategy at the time—happening uncontrollably at the subtle neurological level—but carrying this self-repression and self-loathing into and throughout adulthood was distinctly maladaptive.

The first time I turned the light of my dawning understanding of attachment theory onto myself as a mother, I wanted the earth to open up and swallow me whole. In my then still-typical self-deprecating fashion, I thought immediately of the times I'd failed to respond appropriately to my son's needs, felt racked with guilt, and thought, *Well, I messed him up for life.* Thankfully, my MSC training kicked in, and I comforted myself for the pain and provided some needed perspective. *Remember, Laurie, you don't have to be perfect; that's an old pattern you can let go of. There is the concept of "good enough," and Eric can rewire.* I also allowed myself to recall times when my son had exhibited obvious resilience in the face of great challenge and to entertain the idea that I might possibly have had something to do with helping him develop that quality. I concluded that I had done a better job of parenting than my mother, who had done a better job than hers, who had done a better job than hers. . . . I celebrated that progress and the fact that Eric, should he choose to have a child, would do a better job than I.

You can imagine my eyes opening wider as the implications of all these learnings sunk in. Of course, I'd had a sense for years of my having childhood issues that I believed I needed to get over by feeling my feelings or talking them through; it drove me into therapy periodically throughout adulthood. Now, however, it became a much more nuanced understanding of the depth to which I had been affected by what had happened to me early on in life and of the primacy I would need to give the body in my healing. But it wasn't just the personal that my eyes were opening to. I began to see trauma and its devastating effects everywhere, in seemingly everyone's story, in everyone's body, in my family members, in people in my social circles, in my culture, and in the world. I began to wonder if anyone escapes trauma, if we're all shaped by it, if it's intrinsic to our species. And, I mused, *Shouldn't we be talking about this?*

The final puzzle sidepiece I was working on was the concept of epigenetics. It further upended my worldview and helped prepare fertile ground for somatic therapy and my overall healing. Before stumbling on this information—exactly how I don't remember—I, like most of my chronological peers perhaps, understood that my genes determined who I was, including my state of health. Those pesky, chronic symptoms I mentioned earlier? My father's whole side of the family suffered with similar issues, so I'd accepted it as my genetic destiny. But along comes this relatively new science of epigenetics (*epi*, from the Greek for "upon, besides, attached to, over," take your pick), and it turns out the picture isn't that simple. The science is quite complex, and I don't yet grasp it completely, despite my being a bit of a geek. The biggest takeaway from my brief exposure is that external and environmental factors can unequivocally affect whether genes ever get turned on for things like disease and that this has a multigenerational effect.

Here I was again, with yet another sign pointing to the same truth: elements outside myself, which I had no control over at the time, had profoundly shaped who I understood myself to be. Instead of feeling depressed or angry, though, I felt strangely soothed because it was clear that my experience was nothing unique. It was just the human experience, built right into our design, for better or for worse. There would be no downside to this design if we were all raised by flawlessly well-adjusted, fully self-aware, superbeings. But that's just not the case. We're all raised by completely human, variously damaged folks with greater or lesser degrees of wounding and unconsciousness, and that fact has profound implications for each of us and for society as a whole.

As I completed this final side section and slotted it into the main body of my life puzzle, I felt incredibly hopeful. All the resources and learnings I've written about here shared the emphatic assertion that none of the early damage done was irreversible. None of the patterns laid down, trauma responses wired in, or coping mechanisms adopted had to stay. They might have served me once, but if they no longer did—and most of my early ones clearly didn't—I could discard them and consciously replace them with healthier, more self-supporting, more life-affirming ways of relating to myself, others, and the world. I had discovered that early childhood trauma does not constitute a life sentence. Resilience can be cultivated. Hallelujah!

CHAPTER 6

Coming Alive through Facing Trauma

Trauma bears paying attention to. I can stake my life on that assertion, quite literally: I contemplated suicide twice in my life, and though I had no awareness of it then, I now know that both times, it was unresolved trauma that took me to the edge of existence. Though the external circumstances of my life surrounding each instance were different, it was the same black hole of internal anguish that drove me there. The same choking tendrils of despair darkening my mood, the same abject hopelessness dominating my thoughts, the same excruciating pain manifesting emotionally and physically. Both times, so cut off from any light by the demons of depression, I could see no end to my misery, and I did not want to go on, not one more moment. I just wanted the torment to end.

I'm one of the lucky ones. I didn't go past the brink. The first time I set out to end my life, in my mid-twenties, I turned the steering wheel at the very last minute before I would have intentionally slammed my little tin can of a VW Bug into a concrete bridge abutment at seventy miles an hour. The second time, at age forty-nine, less dramatically but no less near fatally, I made a desperate phone call to a friend. To this day, I don't know exactly what stopped me in those moments given the unrelenting emotional agony I felt and my desperate desire to escape it, permanently. Sometimes I picture having had an angel on my shoulder. Or I picture that tiny spark of life buried deep inside me as JoJo, the shirker in Dr. Seuss's *Horton Hears a Who!*, making himself known just in the nick of time to save the day. Whatever it was, it's the same thing that kept me going during the other bleak periods I experienced over the years—ones that were deep and dark and painful, but not so bad that I wanted life to stop forever.

When I look back, I can see that when I was very young, a pattern of emotional struggle formed that tracked the seasons. I experienced high energy and buoyancy in the spring and summer, which would occasionally ascend into overdrive and frenzied elation. This was followed by a gradual energy drain and sadness in the fall and winter, which would frequently descend into lethargy and crushing despair. The pattern was disruptive. The collateral damage of multiple strained or ruined intimate relationships, repetitive work-life disruptions, chronic health issues, and intermittent financial problems I experienced in its wake over the years might have led another person to doubt their own well-being. However, this pattern's origins were so early and its growth so subtle and insidious that I never questioned the "normalcy" of how I felt and functioned (or didn't function, in some cases). It was all I had ever known, and besides, no one else had ever suggested to me that something might be amiss. I was so used to my yearly rhythms, I'd assumed they were natural. I'd assumed everyone felt and lived just as I did.

By November 1994, ten months after the birth of my son, however, I couldn't get away with holding on to those erroneous assumptions any longer. Suddenly, someone else's life hung in the balance, and as I slid into the all too familiar blue mood and lassitude of autumn, this time greatly exacerbated by the natural sleep disruption and stresses of early motherhood, I realized I was in big trouble, that *we* were in big trouble. I watched with a growing sense of horror and panic as what little physical energy and stores of happiness I did have slipped away, leaving me an exhausted and sorrowful mess, unable to provide proper care for my precious child.

Of course, my husband was witnessing this with his own sense of anguish and trying to support me as best he could while working full time and dealing with the challenges of early fatherhood. But each day when he came home from his job, instead of joining a happy wife and sweet child as earlier, he now entered a mutual hell. As soon as he came through the door, I'd thrust the solid bundle of my son into his arms—hot salty tears that I'd been working harder and harder to choke back as the day interminably wore on already beginning to leak down my cheeks—saying, "Here, you take him." I'd then disappear into another room to weep and rock with fatigue and misery, desperately wondering what in God's name was wrong with me. Thankfully, united in our pain and acknowledgment that this pattern was not normal or healthy for any of us, it wasn't long before we raised the white flag together. Unsure where else to turn at that time in my life, I booked an urgent appointment with my physician.

So began the medicalization of my life, a phase that lasted twenty-five long years. It started with that first doctor who diagnosed depression and prescribed Prozac for me as soon as I could wean Eric off breast milk. She offered me these words of comfort in the face of my disquiet at a mental health diagnosis: "Depression is a disease, like diabetes. You have a chemical imbalance in your brain and need to take a drug to correct it. There's no shame in taking Prozac, just like there's no shame in taking insulin." In retrospect, the fact that the diagnosis shocked me strikes me as sad. I was so out of touch, so inured to severe dysfunction that when someone named it as such, I was surprised. But what really seems tragic about this recollection is how profoundly comforting I found the doctor's words while they essentially condemned me.

I found relief in being told that there was something wrong with me, and therein lies the allure and danger of the allopathic model unchecked: I now had a way to understand my past, to deal with the present, and hope for the future, but it was predicated on the belief in my innate brokenness. Despite the heavy toll—of which I remained largely in denial until I couldn't be any longer—to my body, mind, and spirit, I invested heavily in that belief over the next couple of decades. So heavily, in fact, that ten years after that first diagnosis of depression, I would accept a new one: bipolar II, where the ups were called hypomanias, not as full blown as with "straight" bipolar. During the time between diagnoses, I had gone through two interstate moves, several different doctors (including my first psychiatrist), and various antidepressant cocktails, and I still couldn't seem to handle life's challenges well enough. So, my thinking was, *Oh, okay, this finally explains it. BP II is what's really wrong with me. Antidepressants just were not enough.*

This may sound odd, and it comes with the benefit of hindsight, but I'm thankful that this new diagnosis brought an exponentially higher price for investing in the belief in my own innate brokenness because it jumpstarted the end of that belief for me. With a mood stabilizer now added to my pharmaceutical mix, the side effects became more complex and virulent, including dry mouth, gum recession, loss of libido, anorgasmia, exacerbated insomnia, and weight gain. Lifestyle issues also arose, like being tied to the clock so that I could take doses at precise times of day and night to avoid "breakthrough" symptoms. I recall too many dinner parties where I'd furtively set a timer on my phone, then scurry off to the bathroom to take a pill when the alarm quietly sounded. I also had to be careful with food. Even though I loved grapefruit and enjoyed having them for breakfast, I'd had to give them up because of their harmful interaction with one of my drugs. What I was doing to be "sane" was starting to feel crazy.

In the face of that feeling, I did what perhaps everyone in my shoes has done at one point: I tried an alternative way of treating my problem. While a voice in my head was whispering to me, *There's got to be a better way*—which I now see as evidence that my core self was alive and well in there somewhere—my awareness of trauma and undertaking of its healing still lay far off in the future. So, my approach to choosing an alternative at this point constituted more an act of desperate fleeing from something odious rather than a conscious turning toward something viable. Caught in the black-and-white thinking that's one of the legacies of trauma, I just wanted out of the allopathic nightmare I felt trapped in and assumed anything holistic was the answer.

On the other side of healing, with its benefits of greater wisdom and fresh perspectives, I now see health care in a much more nuanced, shades-of-gray way. I've adopted an integrative approach, blending the best of allopathic and holistic understandings and modalities, depending on the issue. If I get hit by a truck, like my husband did, I'm glad they'll take me to a trauma center and not to an acupuncturist. However, if I'm dealing with something less acute and suspect an emotional component, I'm going to first look to an energy medicine practitioner if I feel I need outside support in my healing.

Back in 2007, though, I had stumbled on homeopathy as an effective way to help my dog with some health issues that weren't responding to traditional veterinary care, and I naively jumped to the conclusion that it would also work for me. I never even paused to assess the vast difference in nature and complexity between canine allergies and human mental health. While homeopathy's usefulness in some situations is laudable (I'm a big fan of how homeopathic zinc can shorten the duration of or even wipe out the common cold), my attempt to apply it in this instance backfired in a catastrophic way when I impetuously turned myself over to a homeopathic physician. He weaned me off pharmaceuticals, prescribed a course of various remedies, and all seemed to go well at first. But after about a month, absolute chaos began to reign, and it became clear that dropping the drugs had been too quick and less than skillful; the doctor's holistic prescription was not working.

My system went haywire: For three agonizing months, I couldn't sleep, at all; my nights were a torment of repeated abortive attempts to sink into oblivion; my days were spent beyond exhaustion and in a horrifyingly mixed state of simultaneous hyperarousal and brain fog; I cried almost constantly and could barely perform the normal functions of daily living. Nothing the physician and I tried seemed to help, and as I grew increasingly frantic to stop the suffering, I reached that second brink I mentioned earlier. Chillingly alarmed when I started to think of specific ways to end my life, I called my closest friend who came right away, essentially saving my life. With her insistence and assistance, I crawled back to my prior psychiatrist and began a protracted and desperate effort to regain stability under that doctor's expert and compassionate care. Ironically, I ended up on more pharmaceuticals than I'd been on before I tried to get off them, and some of the new ones were scary powerful and had side-effect profiles that made my previous list seem totally benign.

So, there I was in late 2015, seven years into having chastenedly reaccepted my fate as someone who required prescription psycho-active drugs to function, resigned to being a mail-order pharmacy customer for life, when I hit the pool wall with my head, altering my life irrevocably. The most profound change came a little over a year after that accident, during my mindfulness and compassion training with their associated learnings about neuroscience and trauma, when I bumped into something else: A simple question—

one that offered a completely new paradigm of mental health. A paradigm that starts not by asking, "What's wrong with you?" but rather, "What happened to you?" On the surface, the difference may not seem significant, but this flip of inquiry represents a radical shift.

The first paradigm bases itself on a belief in innate brokenness, the second in innate wholeness. Under the spell of the first, I had accepted that I was born with a defective brain that needed an external substance to fix it. Now, fully immersed in the realm of the second, I understand that I began whole, that outside forces shaped the conditioning of my brain, and that I have the power to heal it. I can de-condition, re-condition, and self-condition my way back to that wholeness. I now understand that for me there is no such thing as "mental" health, just health, which is an inside job that starts with the nervous system.

Of course, I didn't grasp the truth of all this right at the start, or all at once. It's been a process of getting intimate with myself and then with my trauma—personal, familial, ancestral, and cultural—and how it has been living in my body and shaping my life. I started this journey of intimacy in earnest when I began trauma-specific therapy in August of 2018. After searching the Somatic Experiencing website for trained practitioners in my area and conducting a few interviews, I settled down to exploration with Gloria Gonzalez. The work we've done together over the years, though informed by SE, is profoundly shaped by Gloria's unique background in Chinese medicine theory, Iyengar yoga, Organic Intelligence, Nia, visceral manipulation, craniosacral therapy, and various other somatic modalities, as well as by her own brilliant model of transformation, I AM The Medicine, which is based in Chinese medicine 5 Element theory. Gloria's is a beautiful mix, a crazy quilt of healing powers, that inspires a deeper listening through the body, imprints a greater wholeness, and encourages higher potential through a sense of purpose and life path. When people ask me what my trauma therapy looks like, I sometimes struggle to describe what we actually do together. However, one thing is crystal clear: unlike in my many previous courses of strictly talk therapy, which were only helpful to a degree, my body and nervous system are the focus here, and I have finally experienced fundamental change.

This core transformation started with the SE method's different way of understanding not only my lifelong emotional highs and lows but also many of my other symptoms. Instead of identifying them as evidence of an inborn broken brain or body, SE views them as the manifestations of unresolved traumatic stress. I'll never forget the deep, visceral feeling of *yes* when, early on in our work together, Gloria showed me this brilliant diagram:

SYMPTOMS OF UN-DISCHARGED TRAUMATIC STRESS
©2021 Somatic Experiencing International

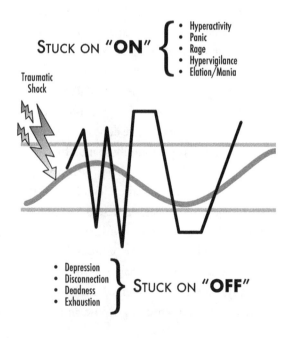

See the jagged black line? It perfectly depicts my life before medication: the exaggerated fluctuations of a nervous system either hyperaroused or shut down—stuck on or stuck off—the "offs" being more profound than the "ons" in my unique manifestation. Originally, I had accepted this pattern as normal, and then I had dutifully pathologized it just as allopathic medicine bid me. Now, I could see that it was neither normal nor pathological but perfectly natural—perfectly understandable—given the things that had happened to me and the circumstances of my upbringing. I simply had a dysregulated nervous system. The good news was that I could learn how to regulate it, bring it back to the undulating gray sine wave between the lighter gray parallel lines, to the normal highs and lows of a well-regulated nervous system. And I didn't have to settle for a drug-flattened wave. (If I were to remake this diagram in my own image at the time I began therapy with Gloria, I'd have to add a straight line running down the middle. Stable, but rather lifeless.)

For the most part, that lovely sinuous sine wave reflects my life pattern now. I say "for the most part" because even after almost three years of therapy, mild symptoms of dysregulation still arise from time to time. Instead of rejecting them, though, I welcome them as a sign that I'm bumping up against yet another place of trapped energy that needs to be integrated or a bit of old wiring that needs replacing. For example, when insomnia showed up near the end of 2020. At the time, mask-wearing and physical distancing still ruled but absolute lockdown had been lifted, and I planned to go on solo retreat to a friend's remote cabin in Lone Pine, California. It was a trip I'd conceived of and arranged for myself to work on editing this book in hopes of pursuing publication, but I toyed with not going, musing that maybe this old, familiar sleeping issue was a sign from my body that I should stay put.

Recognizing the old pattern of nervous system activation and wanting to understand what it could mean, I began to play in my mind with the reasons it might be showing up. Maybe it was COVID nervousness? It would be the first time I'd traveled in many months, suddenly increasing my chances of exposure to the virus. Maybe it was about the destination? I knew that Lone Pine could be fiercely windy and bone-scorchingly dry—two climatological phenomena that in the past had tended to wear me down or set me on edge. A few other possible explanations came to me, but none of them rang quite true in my gut. So, I turned to my journal and then to discussion with my husband to help me figure it out.

In the end, I realized that my body was indeed trying to keep me from going, but through a pattern of protectiveness born from old wounding that had nothing to do with my current reality. In the past, it had not been safe for me to live fully (remember the clamshell I held in the picture?), and I'd developed an unconscious habit of self-abnegation that was arising now. The writer's retreat I'd arranged for myself, as a step toward putting a book out into the world, represented my daring to show up in life more completely. So, my body—remembering old repetitive hurtful consequences—was trying to keep me small and quiet, trying to keep me from getting hurt yet again. After coming to this realization and thanking my body for its previous defensive service, I got in my car and hit the road, knowing that in taking this conscious action, I was effectively rewiring my neural network with a new message: The adult me is in charge now; it's safe for me to live with energy, reach for what I want, and pursue my dreams. I resumed sleeping well that very night.

Traumatic stress that has been ignored for sixty-plus years doesn't get resolved quickly. I've found the process to be a layered one. Each time I cleared old pain from my system, I would go through a period of integration and peace, filled with blessed days, weeks sometimes, of steady regulation. The first few times that happened, I naively thought, *Okay, I'm done, I'm healed,* but then dysregulation would hit again, and an even more painful wound would arise for me to work with. Slowly, I grasped the organic nature of the process. I surrendered to it, realizing that each cycle of surfacing, release, and integration left me stronger, healthier, and more alive and with greater capacity, skills, and resources to meet what would inevitably come up next on the way to greater well-being.

And come up it does. As my therapist loves to say, "We don't have to look back to find trauma. It'll surface in the present." The truth of that statement ties into wholeness. With infinite wisdom, our body/mind/spirit will recreate circumstances that touch our traumatic wounds, over and over if need be, until we pay attention to those wounds—until we fully process the stuck energy and return our being to its natural homeostasis. Only then will we live differently.

For example, at age sixty, I healed a shoulder injury that had plagued me for years by finally working through—somatically—my unsuccessful attempt to fight off rape at age twenty. You might find this hard to believe, but I didn't actually name it as rape back when it happened. To me, it was just another in a long line of hurtful, confusing, shame-inducing sexual experiences of various flavors and intensities that had begun in my very early years and that I'd learned—through familial and cultural messaging—to assume were my fault somehow. So, at the time, I tucked it away, numbed myself to it, even complied with my perpetrator's request of "don't tell your daddy"—he being a friend of my father. It wasn't until ten or so years after the incident that a nascent awareness of its true nature began to dawn on me, and I finally, hesitantly, told the story for the first time, naming it outright to someone I trusted. I have since wondered if the rape, even though I was still burying its pain back then, might have been a compelling factor in my deciding, not long after its occurrence, to enter into my first marriage—at the very young age of twenty-two—maybe as a desperate unconscious grab at safety.

In her book on sexuality, *Come as You Are*, Emily Nagoski quotes victim advocate and former police officer Tom Tremblay characterizing rape as "the most violent crime a person can survive." Nagoski follows up by adding, "Those who have not been sexually assaulted can perhaps most clearly understand the experience of a survivor by thinking of them as having survived an attempted murder that used sex as the weapon." I can now recall the incident, stand in the truth of these descriptions for myself, and think rationally about the impact on my life, but a cognitive understanding is never enough. I had to work it through the body.

At the time of the original trauma, my body naturally mustered powerful survival energy that propelled my arms to strike out at the perpetrator. That energy got trapped inside my body when he pinned me down, and I—overpowered—instinctively entered the freeze state to endure the violation. Unaware and unsupported as I was at that age, I never completed the cycle, never reregulated that intense energy like a gazelle does when she shakes off after a near-eating by a lion. I unknowingly carried it in my body for nearly four decades. It stayed with me, constellating into increasing pain and disability until I finally heard the message in my post-surgical "frozen shoulder" and began to work with it differently. How very eloquent the body is, if only we listen.

The statement of truth that is the title of Bessel van der Kolk's seminal book about trauma, *The Body Keeps the Score*, echoes Ida Rolf, who said earlier and more idiomatically, "Your issues are in your tissues." And that's the miraculous basis of somatic therapeutic modalities. Along the way, I have released and then integrated the energy that was trapped in my body from the developmental trauma of growing up with active alcoholism in my family (including the special hell of the effects of alcohol on my fetal nervous system) as well as from specific instances of emotional abuse, sexual assault, the rape I mentioned as well as an earlier one, a serious accident, medical trauma, and more. I've also reckoned with a trauma of my mother's that I was unconsciously carrying in my back, the trauma of my paternal grandmother's shock treatments, the trauma of my French Huguenot ancestors' persecution, women's collective trauma accumulated and passed down through the millennia, and more. It was all in there. And now it's not, or is at least much less so. It'll be interesting to see what comes up next.

It's been a radical rebirth. (I almost want to drop the *re* from that word because I've come to a place of aliveness that I never actually felt before due to the poisoning of my system in utero— before I even had the chance to hit the planet.) It's the journey from medicine taker to medicine maker, and it's ongoing. At some point, I know that the therapy work will be done, and, like Livia, Gloria will also disappear, Lao Tzu–like. But given my history of entrenched trauma and my zeal for the work, that may be a long way off yet. Plus, I feel like I'm just beginning to grasp the power of energy and the body's ability to heal itself. I'll be forever grateful to that first allopathic doctor and the subsequent ones, including the last who walked with me through my recent transformation and so expertly weaned me permanently off pharmaceuticals. Those doctors brought the best of their training to bear and gave me their brand of relief so I could soldier on. I might not be here now if not for them. It was the type of medicine I was ready for at the time, but now, I'm ready for a different kind. I think the world may be too.

CHAPTER 7

～

Dancing Is Good Medicine

A s I sit here at my computer, the sweat barely dry from a dance session, it strikes me that despite its being the cause of shutting down my path to teacher training, I have COVID to thank for helping me make the practice of 5Rhythms my very own. Unable to go to in-person classes and quickly approaching Zoom burnout, not too long into lockdown, I began experimenting solo with 5R, clearing a floor space in my home and using music from various teachers' Spotify and Mixcloud lists. That tentative foray quickly developed into an almost daily habit, and I have a strong sense that 5R has helped enormously to keep me sane, balanced, healthy, and hopeful during quarantine and throughout this whole peculiarly stressful time in history. Now, I'm moved to ask, "Why is this true, and how exactly does it help?"

What comes to me as an immediate answer is the word *waves*. The diagram I shared in the last chapter—showing the sine wave of a healthy regulated nervous system—beautifully depicts the natural rhythm of the human life force, and the goal of my somatic therapy with Gloria is to return me to that flow. As I've come to understand 5R founder Gabrielle Roth's work, that was essentially her same intent. With astonishing acuity, everywhere Roth looked, she saw how energy flows in waves. She saw it in nature, in the bodies of her students, in the movement of emotions, in the cycles of life itself. She identified five stages to every wave, each with its own distinctive rhythm—naming them *flowing*, *staccato*, *chaos*, *lyrical*, and *stillness*—and showed how music could express their unique energetic qualities. She also understood how energy could get stuck and how music and movement could be used as tools to free it, and built the 5R form around these keen insights.

It seems to me that this is the brilliance of the form: Every time a dancer takes to the floor and does a Wave, as one cycle through all five of the rhythms is called in the vernacular of the practice, moving to the offered music, they dance the sine pattern. They embody it, and, as neuroscience teaches us, through sheer repetition of that experience essentially encode it into their body, which is why 5R, while not therapy, is highly therapeutic. As I do 5R, over and over, it's teaching my nervous system exactly what the natural sinuous ups and downs of a well-regulated life feel like, erasing the feel of the trauma-induced violent spikes and troughs of my past, those awful places I used to get stuck. Dancing 5R, especially so frequently these days, has strengthened me for the unrelenting storm of COVID. Through utter familiarity, I can better ride the waves of the pandemic with steadiness and calm, and I'm so grateful that I found the practice before this unruly tempest hit.

I started doing 5R only four months after beginning somatic trauma therapy, and I now understand more fully how the two modalities have gone hand-in-hand, enriching each other so powerfully they're almost indistinguishably entwined in my growth, both belonging in the main body of my healing puzzle. A few times during the two years of every-other-week polyvagal-informed therapy I've done with Gloria, she has remarked on what she perceives as the rapidity of my progress, given that I essentially lived in the freeze state of our human fight/flight/freeze response to danger for over sixty years. I now know in my heart that the reason for the relative speed of my thaw must have much to do with my practice of 5R. While I acknowledge both my own courage and perseverance in the work, I also celebrate the infinite wisdom of the Universe in crossing my path with Gabrielle Roth's at just the right moment.

I never had the privilege of meeting Gabrielle—she died in 2012, six long years before I began the therapeutic piece of the wake-up journey I've been describing in these pages—but I feel like I know her and that she knows me. Among students of her dance practice, I don't think I'm alone in that feeling, and therein lies her special genius. She dove so personally into the mysteries of life and the human experience, with her whole body, heart, soul, and mind, that she arrived at the universal.

She took her journey through movement, music, theater, Gestalt, massage, shamanism, and more, but mainly through the dance. In creating 5R, Roth eschewed set steps, wanting the individual to tune into their own experience and move how their body begs to be moved, but through a loosely prescriptive musical formula, grounded the dance in the sine wave—that foundational energy running through everyone and everything. In so doing, she left behind a path that, for any dancer who takes to the floor, is uniquely their own and simultaneously an experience of the ultimate oneness with others and the energy of life. I'm so grateful that I have the gifts of her audio recordings, videos, and books, as well as the numerous amazing people who are sustaining the lineage after her passing, to help me on my own journey.

I first became acquainted with 5R quite by accident. Well, was it really an accident? Probably not, because, as I've said before, as I've journeyed, it's become increasingly common for whatever will aid my healing to show up in my life in a synchronistic way. I know I didn't find 5R on purpose. It came to me through grace. I happened upon it while engaging in something else, specifically in Mindful Self-Compassion. Even though I had found the MSC online experience to be profound and life changing, it lacked something that was important to me—live human contact. And upon finishing it, I decided that someday I would like to take an in-person version, anticipating the inevitable richness of exploring growth in physical, not just virtual, community with others. When I'd mentioned this desire to Livia, she wholeheartedly encouraged me to consider the five-day MSC Intensive taught at the Esalen Institute in Big Sur, California, every December by the founders of MSC themselves, Neff and Germer. I signed up eagerly.

In December of 2018, only four months after beginning therapy with Gloria, I journeyed to Esalen with the sole aim of deepening my understanding and practice of MSC, but the whole experience—and its significance for my life—went way beyond that original intention. Just being at Esalen proved to be profoundly nurturing. Perched on a magnificent bluff in wild Big Sur, with the pounding surf of the Pacific directly below and the rugged Santa Lucia Mountains rising immediately behind, its landscape first took my breath away, then wrapped me in its warm embrace. Everywhere I looked, there was natural beauty in abundance. Add to that backdrop mouth-watering meals (with much of the produce grown on-site), hot springs baths to soak in, healing massage, fascinating new people to converse with—the very act of living there for those days was an exercise in self-compassion.

And, of course, the workshop itself—the whole reason I was at that magical place—was transformative. Germer and Neff proved to be consummate teachers, remarkable not only for their wisdom and deftness at communicating it, but also for their humor and humanity. The safe space they adroitly established and held throughout our time together created an intentionally compassionate community that was heart-warming to be a part of. I was correct in thinking in-person work around a concept so profound would afford a fuller experience. For example, asking for and receiving a hug from a sharing partner filled me in a warm way that on-screen interaction never could. To top it off, being there gave me the opportunity to actually meet face-to-face with a lovely man I'd been journeying online with for months in one of Kristy Arbon's Somatic Self-Compassion groups, and who has since become a dear soul-friend. At the time I wondered, *How could it get any better than this?*

But it did. On the last full day of the course, the teachers announced that they wouldn't be presenting any formal program that night but instead would be offering anyone who was interested the opportunity to dance, in honor of the fact that we were meeting at Esalen, the birthplace in the 1970s of a particular form of conscious freeform dance called 5Rhythms. They told us that, while we would not be formally practicing 5R because none of the MSC teachers was a certified instructor, the music we would be dancing to had been compiled by one and made available for public use. They suggested we treat the experience as a mindful self-compassion practice set to music, a way to be lovingly present to our own body and how it wants to move without thinking about performance. They assured us that anyone of any ability could participate and encouraged us to "Come if it sounds like fun."

It sounded like a blast, so I went. Looking back, I feel such gratitude for the healing work I'd done before this chance presented itself. Even just a year earlier, still bound up in fear and self-consciousness, I probably wouldn't have honored my desire to participate nor possessed the courage to go. I'm sure the invitation would have piqued my interest because, from early on in my life, I've loved to dance. Over the last few decades, though, I'd pretty much stifled that impulse. My husband never cared much for dancing, so in another of my twisted attempts to "fit in" or accommodate someone else (even though he himself never asked this of me), I'd completely dropped dancing from my life. Before that ripe moment at Esalen, I might have stayed stuck in that place of self-denial. Instead, because I'd come far enough in my trauma recovery, I felt delight in the opportunity and allowed myself to seize it—acknowledging the butterflies of nervousness in my belly while following the energy of love with curiosity.

What I found on the dance floor that night transcended fun, though I did experience plenty of that. I also discovered a freedom of expression, a sense of the energy of life, a connection with myself and others, a renewed feeling of vitality, and an upwelling of joy— lots of sheer, unbridled joy. The music and dance lasted forty-five minutes, and by the end, with sweat pouring off me, I felt exhausted but also exhilarated, bubbling with excitement. Around the giant circle we closed with that night, the reflections folks shared echoed my own experience, and more. Turned out, people had encountered all sorts of things on that dance floor. As individuals and as a collective, we had gone through something. Something big. Even so, except to exchange enthusiastic pleasantries about it with others who'd danced, I didn't pay the experience much more attention as the MSC course wrapped up the next day and I headed home.

Apparently, though, it had wholly lodged itself within me— in my body and soul. As the ensuing days and weeks went by, engaged in "real life" back home, my mind kept returning to the memory of the dance. This happened more and more frequently, until I finally realized that I wanted, almost needed, to experience more of it. I decided to check out the actual practice of 5R, as the MSC teachers had suggested we do, and turned to Google to investigate. When I landed on the 5R website, I was instantly drawn to this paragraph: "Energy moves in Waves. Waves move in patterns. Patterns move in rhythms. A human being is just that—energy, waves, patterns, rhythms. Nothing more. Nothing less. A dance." Intrigued, I pored over all the site's pages and was thrilled to find a class being offered right here in San Diego, held at a community dance space only twenty minutes away from where I live.

About one month after my serendipitous exposure at Esalen, I began my journey with 5R practice in earnest by attending my first official class, and as I drove toward it, I sensed those same butterflies—nervousness plus excitement—that I had experienced originally. I also carried a certain tentativeness within me because the class was scheduled for two hours, and I wondered if I had the stamina. Just my forty-five-minute introduction had tired me out. Plus, in the early stages of my healing, I still had some musculoskeletal issues that I wanted to be careful of. Mostly, though, as I steered my car along the 805 freeway, I felt brave and empowered to give myself permission to dance, to do this thing that called to me and that I had ignored for so many years.

I'll never forget entering the dance studio that day. First, at the door I encountered the genuine and gentle warmth of the bearlike man named Jake, who, I learned months later, is married to the teacher. Then I entered the calm and cradling beauty of the space itself, receiving ready smiles and nods of acknowledgment from the dancers who had arrived before me and already taken to the floor to warm-up. And finally, I soaked in the lively and lovely presence of Christina Graham-Smith, the teacher, who, when I gave her my name and expressed my uncertainty about the class length, put me at immediate ease with a tender embrace and words of encouragement to listen to myself and to do what was right for me. I swear to God, I felt like I was being welcomed home.

After that first class, I started dancing 5R regularly—in San Diego when I was home or in cities I traveled to—and that feeling of homecoming deepened. I felt it in the openness and acceptance of my fellow journeyers who were choosing to find and move their truth through the dance. *This is my crew.* I felt it when I'd come into a studio that had been lovingly and artfully prepared for 5R. *This is my place.* I felt it in the music, which was always inspiring and often surprising, unfailingly touching something eternal within me as I moved to it. *This is what I am meant to do.* But mostly, I felt it in my body, in my very bones, muscles, sinews, organs, heartbeat, breathing. From the moment the soles of my bare feet first touched the floor, through the entirety of the dance, and into the sharing circle when we were all done, I'd come home to myself—my truest nature as a unique human, moving to the beat of the Universe. *This is who I am.*

That sense of being at home in my body, of having dropped into it to a degree I never had before—a sense first awakened in earnest through the body scan practice in Mindfulness-Based Stress Reduction—has grown ever stronger through the consistent practice of 5R, especially now that I dance so often on my own. Thanks to its combining mindfulness with movement, I can now stay tuned in to my body more of the time, not just when I'm sitting still or lying quietly. I can hear what it's saying to me, sense what energies it needs to unblock, recognize what emotions are arising in it, understand what it needs, no matter what I'm doing—interacting with others, exercising, cleaning the house, walking to my car, sitting here writing. I no longer live solely in my head, as if what's real can only be known from the neck up, as if I were merely my thoughts dragging around an uncooperative corporeal anchor. Nope. I *am* my body, only experiencing the fullness of this human existence within and through it.

In creating 5R, Roth built brilliant maps for purposely moving the body, heart, mind, soul, and spirit through the rhythms into greater wholeness, into a state of integration. Almost as soon as I started practicing regularly, I began to experience glimpses of this blessed state. At first, only for the briefest of moments, at tantalizingly transcendent points in the dance. Now, I experience that sense of unbrokenness for increasingly longer stretches of time, on and off the dance floor, and I know, in part, it's because I have moved so much. In the two years I've been playing in the energetic field of 5R, I've danced my way through hundreds of hours of classes, probably just as many now on my own, and days and days of workshop exploration—adding up to almost countless Waves—and I have found a lot more of Roth's promised wholeness. But it has taken discipline and has not always been easy.

Sometimes, I've shown up to the dance with the intent of simply enjoying the experience and seeing what arises. That spirit of playfulness always yields surprises and brings rich pleasure. Sometimes I've shown up specifically to celebrate being in community with fellow journeyers. That connection is always life affirming, and I leave feeling buoyed by it. Sometimes, though, I've dragged myself to the dance with only the idea of getting through it; for example, the time I went to class with debilitating back pain, which had arisen as I worked with Gloria through the unprocessed trauma of a terrible water-skiing accident that had occurred in my twenties.

I vividly remember the deep listening it took that day to stay within a range of motion that was comfortable for my body, to not abandon myself and push past the pain—a habit I'd developed to my detriment as a lifelong competitive athlete. I allowed myself to simply lie on the floor during the *chaos* rhythm and let the vibrations from the driving beat of the music and the many pounding feet roll up my spine, experiencing how simultaneously soothing and enlivening that sensation was. My back issue resolved a short time later, just days after the class, alchemized not only by what I physically sensed moving through me as I lay on the floor, but also by the more intangible medicinal field created by the collective energy of the dancers, who, to a one, show up in service to healing for themselves and others. Do not underestimate the transformative power of intention, especially shared.

One of the most profound experiences I've ever had on the dance floor occurred in the summer of 2019 when I showed up to a five-day 5R workshop at Esalen with a very specific intention. By then, I'd been working in somatic therapy for about a year and had made some good progress in understanding my trauma history and how to work with my body to heal it. As the time for the workshop neared, though, old programming came to the fore, and in session with Gloria I complained, "Wouldn't you know, my hip is bothering me, and I leave for Esalen this Sunday." She enthusiastically responded, "Oh good!" flipping my perspective on its head—from dismay to curiosity. When she followed up by asking what I would like to set as an intention for my time there, a clear answer came to me immediately. "I want to listen carefully to my hip and see what it's trying say to me," I told her.

On the very first day of the workshop, when the teacher, Lucia Horan, spoke specifically about trauma and how it shows up in the body and can be moved, I knew I had come to the right place. I sensed they would probably be five fruitful days, and, sure enough, they were. As I danced through Wave after Wave, with and for my hip, listening so very deeply, I encountered the trauma of rape once again—unsurprisingly, in retrospect. Whereas my frozen shoulder had harbored undischarged energy from my thwarted fight response, I found that the pain and tightness in my hip spoke loudly of my blocked flight response. In addition to trying to push my attacker away, I had struggled desperately to flee from him. But I'd been unsuccessful—legs also pinned in place—and that specific stuckness needed clearing and integrating too.

As the music moved me, I danced through the fear, anger, and grief, exaggerating the movements of kicking and running, flying with fierce energy throughout the huge room filled with moving bodies, shaking free the locked-up power, growling, crying, staying with it . . . dancing, dancing, dancing with awareness. Drenched in the salt of sweat and tears, I came out the other side into a place of such purity and lightness, my muscles loose, all the pain and tightness gone from my hip. I'd catalyzed a profound cleansing, an unimaginable healing, and as my heart swelled with gratitude, it whispered its desire into my ear, "I want to become a 5R teacher so I can help others find life-giving transformation in this exquisite practice." Startled, and then succumbing to a louder inner voice concerned about my age, I tucked away that revelation.

Its exile lasted only briefly. During the closing dance of the workshop, Lucia invited anyone who considered themselves an elder to come to the center of the nearly 100-person moving circle. Responding to what I can only describe as the palpable aura of love and honor behind that invitation, I strode into the middle space, together with a handful of other men and women, claiming my membership in that life category in a public way I never had before. Clasping hands in an interior circle turned out to face the larger one, we occupied pride of place as the rest of the community danced around us, looking each of us in the eyes and showering us in gratitude and respect with their expressions, their gestures, their whole bodies, their hearts. While I received this holy blessing of my elderhood, tears of joy streamed down my cheeks, a grin split my face, and tiny sobs escaped my throat as I exulted in being a crone. In having made it this far. In having acquired wisdom. In having so much still to give. In being seen and appreciated for all of that—instead of being dismissed as my inner voice had tried to do.

At lunch later that day, I had a quick opportunity to thank Lucia for her purposeful ritual of recognition of us elders. Her gracious accepting of my appreciation was coupled with a lovely matter-of-factness, as if to say, "Well, of course, why wouldn't we want to honor the elders?" Right then, in the sunshine of her frank regard, I sensed a blossoming of my desire to teach, and suspected that my gray head and advanced years would not be seen as impediments in the 5R community. I later confirmed that suspicion when, back home in San Diego, I booked an online session with Lucia and shared my wish with her. Both she and Christina, my local teacher, have been nothing but encouraging to me in my journey toward possibly teaching one day, and I consider myself richly blessed to have them as mentors.

At the end of *Maps to Ecstasy*, Gabrielle Roth's book detailing her vision behind the 5R practice, she boldly states, "Disease is inertia. Healing is movement. If you put the body in motion, you will change. You are meant to move: from *flowing* to *staccato*, through *chaos* into *lyrical*, and back into *stillness* from which all movement comes. . . . I know that if a wave of energy is allowed to complete itself, it yields a whole new wave, and in fact that is all I really know." Reading her words, I find myself thinking of Peter Levine's words from his book *Waking the Tiger*: "Traumatic symptoms are not caused by the 'triggering' event itself. They stem from the frozen residue of energy that has not been resolved and discharged; this residue remains trapped in the nervous system where it can wreak havoc on our bodies and spirits. . . . Fortunately, the same immense energies that create the symptoms of trauma, when properly engaged and mobilized, can transform trauma and propel us into new heights of healing, mastery, and even wisdom." Is it any wonder I can't quite separate out the impact of 5R from that of somatic therapy on my process of transformation?

I don't know if these two visionaries ever knew each other. It's quite possible they did, given that they were born only a year apart, orbited the same free-spirited and fruitful world of California in the 1960s and 1970s, and shared such similar views of life and the healing journey. Both championed embodiment as the key to well-being and developed potent tools to free up vital energy, reclaim one's true authentic self, and move through life with grace and resilience. A dynamic duo. Even if they never met, I like to imagine this pair of groundbreaking healers hanging out together, swapping insights, and supporting each other's work. I also like to picture them cheering me on as I more and more expertly ride the waves of life, sharing a high five with each other to acknowledge their mutual genius and to celebrate another person released from past trauma, another soul restored to the fullness of herself and returned to the world.

CHAPTER 8

Trauma: It's a Family Affair

It's Mother's Day 2020, and, in true pandemic-style, I park myself in front of my laptop and log on to Zoom so my son and I can videochat. It's one of only a handful of times we haven't been physically present with one another on this holiday. Obviously, it was easy to be together when Eric was younger and lived in our house. And then over the last eight years, Mother's Day often coincided with one of the times each year that my husband and I would visit Eric in Tucson. Not this year, however. Under a shelter-in-place order, a trip to Arizona wasn't even conceivable. As with much of life under the shadow of COVID, this year was going to be different, but not just because of the cyber-nature of our contact.

When Eric's image appeared on the screen, my heart, which always swells with joy on seeing his beloved face, was also pierced with a raw grief.

"Hi, honey," I managed to say with a smile, despite the lump in my throat.

"Hi, Mom! Happy Mother's Day!" He beamed back enthusiastically.

He was wearing one of my favorite shirts of his—a soft pink T-shirt with large, lovely, stylized rose blossoms in shades of deeper salmon and mint green all over it—without the slightest bit of irony. This giant of a man I had somehow long ago given birth to, who topped out at six foot two and two hundred pounds, sports lumberjack facial hair tinged with the red of warrior Norse ancestors, possesses a towering intellect, and speaks in a deep resonant voice, was perfectly at home in the lush flower garden adorning his torso. Eric inhabits his imposing presence comfortably, right along with the tenderest of hearts, ready access to all his emotions, a fierce affinity for any underdog, and the ability to weep unapologetically when moved, which is easily. He is a wonderfully integrated human, one of my greatest teachers in this life, a person who naturally embodies the yin/yang principle, equally at home with his own masculine and feminine energies.

It is my astonishing good luck to be his mother, and here he was, on screen, eager to spend time with me. During some small talk, I took in the full wonder of the planes of his face—the deep-set brow he inherited from his dad, the prominent chin he inherited from me, and all the other angles that are his very own and come together to make him unique. Then I took a deep breath and began to steer us in another direction. "Hey, honey, there's something I'd like to share with you."

I went on to tell him how, during the week preceding this special Sunday, I had experienced huge movement in my trauma recovery, all centering around being a mother. That movement had been primed by a heartfelt conversation with one of my dearest friends about her grief at estrangement from her daughters following her courageous choice to leave a toxic marriage. Then it had been lit by the match of a therapy session focused on my hellacious experience of giving birth to Eric—strangely enough, the first time I'd dared to apply the word *trauma* to it. And finally, it had been fueled by a 5R workshop on mother energy. I had broken through into a fiery cleansing, into a new, deeper understanding of our shared experience as mother and son.

I told him that, deep in my heart, I felt the need to share this new understanding with him, and Mother's Day seemed like the perfect time to do so, asking if he would be okay with that. He was, so I told him a condensed version of the birth story that follows in this chapter. He had, of course, heard some of the facts before, but never the insights into the whys that had just days earlier coalesced for me. When I finished my tale, which included a heartfelt apology for the harm I had caused him, he paused, looked me squarely in the eye, and said in the softest, most loving voice, "I forgive you, Mom. And I hope you forgive yourself."

Since my healing journey began four years ago, Eric—who is twenty-seven now—and I have had many frank discussions about the turmoil of his early life and my part in it. Each time, he has readily offered me his absolution. I sometimes wonder if he has delved deeply enough into how much I may have wounded him. And as his life unfolds, his perspective on my parenting may change. However, his life is his own, he's a completely different person than I am, and science tells us that what one human experiences as traumatizing another may not. In any case, he has progressed along the path of awakening lightyears beyond where I had at his age, and the fact that he has forgiven me remains one of the greatest graces of my life.

You see, it proved impossible for me to come to grips with—and process—my childhood trauma and not slam into the harsh truth of having perpetrated some of the very same on my own offspring, on the being most precious to me in all the world. Just writing that sentence makes my chest ache. But because facing truth is an important part of living an awakened life, I welcome that pain and am working, on an ongoing basis, to transmute it by practicing self-forgiveness—as Eric has encouraged me to do—for my past foibles and failures. Like right now, this very moment, I'm going to pause my typing, place my hand on my tender heart, and spend a few moments wishing myself peace and remembering that in my life, regardless of the outcome, I have always tried to love as best I could.

More informed now about the precarious nature of child development by my self-study into the subject matter, I fully grasp the stunning import of the complete and utter dependency of the human infant on others for its survival. Unlike many other animals, it's in the design (a flawed one, perhaps?) of *Homo sapiens* that someone else must keep us safe for quite a long time after we're born. This is true not just so we stay alive, but also so we can internalize that sense of safety, the deep interior confidence in the body, mind, and spirit that all is right with our world, and we ourselves are fine. That feeling is our homeostasis, the stable platform we need to stand on to flourish amidst the inevitable vicissitudes of life. We can certainly exist without an internal sense of safety (as I did for so long), but we absolutely cannot thrive without it—as was again obvious in my life. So, what happens if the person who's in charge of a helpless infant doesn't feel safe themselves, as was the case with my mother and then with me? Trauma happens, and it gets passed on unless it's healed.

In their March 26, 2015, online post about Somatic Experiencing therapy in *Psychology Today*, Roger Saint-Laurent and Sharlene Bird presented this brilliantly concise working definition of trauma: "*anything that is too much, too soon, or too fast for our nervous system to handle*, especially if we can't reach a successful resolution." Reading this description switched on a light bulb in my mind, illuminating why my mother's drinking during her pregnancy constituted trauma for me. The developing fetal nervous system is simply unequipped to handle bloodstream alcohol, especially on a repeated basis, so I clearly experienced a case of too much, too soon. And because I was powerless to get away from the intoxicant, the possibility of a successful resolution just did not exist.

I mention this specific trauma from my very earliest life because I see it as my source wound, the place where my generalized sense of unsafety likely originated—before I was even born—and because I passed the same pain on to my own son. My mother's uterus was an intermittently dangerous place to be, and, by not coming to grips with that reality and its repercussions in my own life before becoming pregnant myself, despite not drinking a drop of alcohol during my pregnancy, my womb was too. My source wound—reinforced countless times by various circumstances and events of my upbringing—bred core feelings of helplessness and powerlessness within me. These shaped my perspective and behavior in ways I was totally unaware of and unknowingly carried into impending motherhood, fatefully coloring Eric's origin story.

I shared with Eric that I could now clearly see how this learned way of being played out during pregnancy and childbirth—like in other areas of my life—mainly through ignoring my own internal wisdom and turning my power over to others. To a health-care provider in this case. From the start of my pregnancy, I willingly participated in the dance of "doctor knows best," despite misgivings that arose during my very first visit to the family practitioner I'd chosen. After she informed me of my due date, which she'd calculated based on my last menstrual period, I ventured that I thought I knew the exact moment of conception and had a sense that the due date might be sooner. In response to my apparent gall in challenging the accepted formula, I received a stern lecture about how I couldn't possibly know such a thing, and how her calculus was superior and would guide our game plan. Blindly locked in shame and crippling self-doubt as I was at that time in my life, I acquiesced to her "authority," and in so doing, set the stage for my son's gestational and birth ordeal.

I swam my way through the many months of pregnancy, without morning sickness or fatigue or any of the myriad other difficulties that can plague a woman, but when my uterine contractions began four weeks ahead of the doctor's inviolable schedule (unsurprisingly, in retrospect), the fun was over. Although both the baby and my body knew it was the right time to get the party started, I once again characteristically deferred to the doctor's supposed medical expertise and agreed to a kind of house arrest. I stayed home for two weeks and maintained a horizontal position for as much of the time as possible. More damaging, I also allowed myself to be put on a drug to suppress labor. Now, just like my mother before me, I unconsciously and unintentionally made my body a dangerous place for my unborn child, not only by pumping pharmaceuticals into a fetal nervous system not designed to process them, but also by blocking his innate natural energy toward birth. The drama only grew from there. After those long days of the rest-and-ingest protocol, which disrupted my and my husband's lives significantly, I could stop taking the drugs and move about freely, because now the doctor deemed it "safe" for the baby to be born. (How ironic is that?) Of course, the blessed event didn't happen right away.

Looking back, I'm amazed at the naivete on all our parts—mine, the doctor's, other people's—of expecting things to proceed rapidly, as if nothing difficult had just occurred, as if neither the baby nor I would be affected by our mutual experience of imposed shut down. One of us seemingly voluntarily and one of us clearly not, we had just both been forced into a freeze state for two weeks. It's no wonder that another two whole weeks went by before I felt a contraction again and the birth finally began to unfold. By that time, I was huge. I had gained a total of forty-five pounds—a full 40 percent of my original 110 pounds—and it was practically all in my abdomen. There was a little bit of roundness to my cheeks and limbs that wasn't there before pregnancy, but I essentially looked like a stick figure that had swallowed a watermelon.

At eight pounds fourteen ounces, Eric was quite a bit bigger than the average American newborn, perhaps not remarkable except that, as you probably surmised upon reading my pre-pregnancy weight, I'm a small person. At five seven, I am a few inches above average height for an American woman. But I'm rather delicate-boned and slender-framed (a lifelong size 4, except during the years of my deepest enmeshment with big pharma) with a pelvis better suited to a more average-sized baby—say one born a month earlier? But none of us paid this any heed, as on the evening of December 31, 1993, my husband and I started to attend to the timing of my contractions and excitedly prepare to welcome what we reasonably assumed would be a New Year's Day baby. Boy or girl, we didn't yet know.

It'll come as no surprise at this point that labor and delivery were a horror show. Turned out, it was impossible for Eric to enter the world in the usual way, though I tried valiantly to make that happen. I've blocked much of that day-and-a-half of agony from memory, as a survival mechanism I think, but there are a few vivid flashes that come to me in stark detail. Like one moment of acute degradation involving the hot tub in one of the birthing suites at the community hospital where the drama unfolded. I had immersed myself in the warm, soothing water, hoping for some relief from the unrelenting pain and some assistance in relaxation, to help along what even the doctors and nurses were by then calling an "unusually protracted process." Only minutes after submerging my awkward bulk, a fiercely mounting nausea gripped me. I struggled out of the tub, naked, sweating, and dizzy, only to be racked simultaneously with projectile vomiting and explosive diarrhea, unable to figure out which end of me to point toward the toilet, dazedly twirling in place and filling the small bathroom with my effluvium. I was undone.

But only momentarily. Once cleaned up with the help of my long-suffering husband and an officious staffer, I resumed my tenacious pursuit of natural childbirth, struggling undaunted for many more hours. Unfortunately, I wasn't the only one who struggled that day. The anesthesiologist, called in when I finally relented, bungled the epidural, effectively paralyzing me and adding more time and terror to the ordeal as I waited for the frightening effects of his misjudgment to wear off enough so I could actually push when the time finally came. But that time would never come. After thirty-six hours of titanic effort, unfruitful misery, and mismanaged intervention, my physician finally called it. Having spiked a fever and now shaking uncontrollably, with multiple monitors around me screeching out their rapid rhythmic alarms signaling dangerous levels of maternal and fetal distress, I was rushed on a gurney to an OR, desperately pleading in my delirium, "Just get this baby out of me alive."

Eric was born shortly thereafter via emergency C-section, and the operation was pronounced a success: "Mother and baby are fine." Well, we were both alive, certainly. Eric was healthy and whole, and we were able to bond well once the warm bundle of him was laid on my chest, after I regained consciousness and he'd been checked over. I am eternally grateful for all of that, to be sure. But fine? Really? We had both been through a waking nightmare, as had my husband who was by my side the whole excruciating time. It wasn't just bodily torment we'd experienced. For the adults, it had also been emotionally draining and brutal for the spirit. And where to begin in sorting out how Eric's vulnerable nervous system and whole tiny new being might have been affected?

No special import was given to our experience, though, save for some cursory expressions of dismay from the surgeon and the staff that it "hadn't gone as planned." In the early 1990s, even in Boulder, Colorado—a city perpetually viewed as tuned-in and forward thinking—the idea of processing trauma, or even extreme stress, was still far outside anyone's thinking. So, the entirety of the pain we'd all experienced, much of it survival energy (that I now know needs to be resolved in the body's tissue memory or it will fester into mental or physical symptoms or both), got added to each of our loads. It wouldn't be until over two decades later that I would finally comprehend the vast burden of unhealed wounds I had labored under at that time, and how my unconsciousness about my own trauma dramatically shaped Eric's entry into the world and his early years. This is what I apologized to him for on Mother's Day 2020—and what I received his forgiveness for—but, of course, the story doesn't end there.

Having buried the pain of the previous few days and surrendered to the bliss of oxytocin-fueled new motherhood, I left the hospital about forty-eight hours later, with my newborn son strapped in his car seat in the back of our little gray Mazda 323 and my husband at the wheel, carefully navigating the snow and ice on the roads, the winter sun shining brightly through the thin mountain air. Miraculously, given my previous mental health challenges, I didn't fall prey to postpartum depression, and the first several months of Eric's life, while challenging—as new parenthood always is—were a joyous time for me. The boundless love I felt for this new little human, the awe at our deep connection, and the sheer fun of nurturing his development exceeded my wildest imaginings. I ate it up, having chosen to put aside work outside the home for a few years and devote myself to being a full-time parent, not everyone's choice in contemporary times, but one that felt right for me.

Without younger siblings or cousins or any other previous experience with infants, I had been a little nervous about becoming a mother. Would I know what to do? Would I be any good? So, I was pleasantly surprised at how at ease I felt and how naturally the behaviors came to me—the breast feeding, the diaper changing, the snuggling, the patting of his back when he fussed, the swaying from foot-to-foot that seemed to rise up out of me instinctually from some ancient source as I held him. Through the cold of winter into the bursting spring and beyond, Eric and I reveled in ten great months together, and that fact is my cherished consolation. I cling to the possibility that maybe the deep bonding—the secure attachment, dare I hope—that we achieved during those months was enough to get him through what came next. When, as I shared earlier, the solid ground began to disappear from beneath me as summer turned to fall, and my old seasonal "stuck off" pattern resurfaced in a devastating way.

When I think back on this time in our lives, my heart hurts for my little boy as his mother slipped away from him. He was never in physical danger. Thankfully, abusiveness doesn't dwell in my nature nor my repertoire of learned behaviors. And each day during my decline, I somehow summoned the minuscule stores of energy I still possessed and used them to feed, change and clothe, cuddle, read to, and even play with him—a testimony, I believe, to the astounding power of the maternal drive. (By God, I was going to take care of that boy, even if it killed me.) As the months progressed, that gargantuan effort to stay on board took its toll on me so that by the end of those days, I hung on by a mere thread, barely able to manage even that tearful hello I previously described as I handed Eric over to my husband in the evening.

Neuroscience, developmental psychology, and attachment theory have all taught me that my energetic and emotional withdrawal at that stage in his life had to have deeply impacted Eric. It probably still does to this day and will into his future. I wonder if, for his own well-being, Eric might need to go back and dig into that time—as well as any others of his growing up that were punctuated by my emotional struggles—to uncover any wounding and work on his own healing. I've shared that thought with him. In the end, whether any of these early life experiences constituted trauma for him is a question for Eric alone to ask and answer, should he choose. My task is to continue practicing the self-compassion necessary to live with serenity in the face of my part in his suffering.

Unfortunately, there is one incident from Eric's childhood that undeniably qualifies as trauma—the acute type, absolutely life altering—one that he and I had talked about many times before Mother's Day 2020. It's to that one that I turn now. First, I want to acknowledge that telling this story feels a bit tricky, in the sense that on some level I'm essentially an outsider to it. It happened to Eric and not to me directly, though of course I participated in it. I can't ever know his reality, his experience of the event, and its aftermath. Only he can. He's undertaken some important introspective as well as therapeutic work around this episode, and his understandings of it and its implications for his life belong to him, are his truth. All I can know, tell, and reflect upon is what I experienced as his mother, a not-so-innocent bystander.

Let me set the stage by sharing that, right from the start, Eric seemed to me to have hit the planet like a buddha—happy, calm, and wise—despite the craziness of his last in-utero month and the birth complications. Yes, he cried, and enthusiastically so, when he was hungry, wet, poopy, or tired—as an infant should. But when his needs were met, he was joy and equanimity personified: sparkly-eyed and alert, ready to engage, yet also quietly observant with a deep soulful gaze and content to be held. He retained those underlying qualities as he grew past the newborn phase, through infancy, and into toddlerhood, which began a bit early as he virtually passed over crawling, instead opting at ten months to go almost directly from rolling as his preferred way to get across the floor to walking.

Throughout his first year, a lively curiosity emerged. Seemingly thousands of times a day, like a monosyllabic lamb, he'd bleat out a single inquisitive "Ba?" while pointing to something he wanted identified. And he'd appear to listen carefully to the name of the object and my explanation of its use or significance. A palpable gutsiness appeared as well. First through gestures and sounds, then with actual words, he'd insist on tackling challenges that intrigued him—like the stairs before he could even walk. Then there was his unmistakable zest for life. He played hard, napped harder, always woke up smiling, and ate everything in sight. Eric was easy and fun to be around, which wasn't the opinion of his besotted mother alone.

All that changed, though, over the course of just a few hours when he was fourteen months old. Only about two months after our family's restoration to full functionality with the help of pharmaceuticals, an unidentified life-threatening health crisis that baffled the medical experts at the time swooped in suddenly and without warning to alter Eric's life irrevocably. One minute he was his normal, vibrant, happy self, the next—midstream in one of the infectious belly laughs he was famous for—he was a stunned heap on the kitchen floor, his ivory skin turning a hideous mottled purple, his polar bear romper-clad chest heaving as he struggled to breathe, his eyes wide with terror. The visual of that rapid grotesque transformation is seared into my brain with eerie precision, as are many of the adrenaline-fueled moments that followed in the emergency room. The ghastly scene of Eric lying on his back, kicking and screaming, two nurses forcibly holding him down while another repeatedly stabbed his tiny arm, attempting to insert an IV line as I tried in vain to comfort him, is a mental movie clip that will forever haunt me. This was trauma, with a capital T: too much, too soon, too fast, no resolution. No way to explain to this innocent, trusting child why we were ganging up on him and hurting him, or why I abandoned him when the doctor asked me to leave the room because, in her view, my presence impeded their ability to save my child's life.

Ironically, though I am forever grateful that they did indeed save his life, the way in which the medical staff accomplished it—rapidly, forcefully, automatically, and without a thought to his experience of their intrusive interventions—robbed him of much of it. But I wouldn't face that fact, or fully understand it, for many more years. So overjoyed that Eric had survived his mysterious ordeal, my husband and I brought him home from the hospital a few days later, determined not to dwell on the recent horrors and to put the nightmare behind us. Which we managed to do for a little while, until we couldn't anymore.

It wasn't long before I sensed that, while still recognizably himself, Eric had been fundamentally altered by his experience. Most notably, glimpses of his innate joy and equanimity grew fewer and fainter, replaced instead by mounting debilitating hypersensitivities. Loud sounds startled the previously unflappable boy into panic, rough labels in his clothes irritated him into tears, the mouth feel of many foods revolted the former chowhound. Alongside these and other troubling developments, I watched with confusion and sorrow as a general fearfulness crept into his attitude and behavior, as an inability to sit still replaced his capacity to happily plop down with a picture book or beloved toy and spend long periods contentedly engaged. A marked increase in general health issues—recurring ear infections, blossoming allergies, scary breathing challenges—became his new normal.

A few times through the years, though I wasn't yet acquainted with the idea of trauma nor the language to describe it, I cornered whomever his doctor was at the time and tried to communicate my urgent sense that Eric had been changed—harmed—by his childhood incident. Unfortunately, each time I expressed such an opinion, I was met with either patronizing dismissal or outright disdain. Sometimes a doctor would casually offer a "diagnosis." Terrible Twos early on or

ADHD in second grade are two I remember hearing pronounced but, thankfully, rejecting. Unheard and getting nowhere with these professionals, I did what I knew how to do all too well: I silenced myself. Just like during my pregnancy, I ignored my deep inner knowing, consigning my son to continue in his living hell.

From where I stand now, twenty-six years after the original event, fully informed about trauma and having reclaimed my power, it's hard for me to believe that I was ever that person who repeatedly swallowed her truth and bowed so readily to the authority of others. But I also understand that I was an unaware, unhealed trauma victim myself, and I feel a deep compassion for that unsure, chronically frightened, self-doubting woman who was doing the best she could at the time. Unfortunately, that best caused Eric to suffer mightily an unnecessarily long time in his young life. He lived with a full-blown case of post-traumatic stress disorder for sixteen years before an insightful therapist finally named it. And he could begin to unpack the truth, start to heal, and begin to recover his wholeness.

I remember sitting on the beach, just two and a half years ago, devouring a section from *In Unspoken Voices*, one of Peter Levine's books on trauma, about a Somatic Experiencing intervention he did with a toddler boy following a medical event strikingly similar to Eric's. Levine vividly depicted how they artfully processed the event—using a favorite stuffed animal and play—to release the trapped survival energy and restore the little boy to balance. Oblivious to the joyful shouts of the vacationing families around me, I wept with abandon as I read that passage, realizing that with simple help rendered early on, it would have been possible, even easy, to save Eric from years of agony and struggle.

Perhaps you can see why I assert that trauma is passed on until it's healed. I was utterly incapable of honoring my inner wisdom, persisting in its truth in the face of external resistance, investigating appropriate options, or pursuing timely help for my offspring because I had not yet faced my own experiences of overwhelm and the sense of powerlessness they had melded into my system. Sometimes, I imagine an ideal world where no one would tackle parenthood until they'd cleared their system of all old wounds and rewired themselves completely for presence and resilience. How blessed future generations would be, raised by those folks. But we don't live in an ideal world, do we? More helpful than envisioning the impossible is when I recommit, over and over, to doing my work of waking up and healing and sharing the journey with my son, like I did on Mother's Day. I know in my heart that it's never too late for me to parent better. By doing so I can help him heal and do a better job than I did, should he choose to become a parent himself.

Through my trauma work, I've arrived at a completely different understanding of the nature of raising children. To begin with, I now see it as a privilege, not a right, and I no longer view it as the process of molding and shaping another human being, as social convention defines it. Instead, I conceive of it as the deeply sacred task, to be undertaken with the utmost humility, of keeping them physically, mentally, emotionally, and spiritually safe—first and foremost from ourselves—so that they can grow into the fullness of who they are, who they have come to this Earth already being. My parenting motto: "Want to help your kid? Heal yourself." Apparently, Thich Nhat Hanh agrees with me, because just yesterday I saw this quote of his: "The most precious inheritance that parents can give their children is their own happiness."

Since committing to my own healing—in essence, my own happiness—the relationship I have with my son has blossomed beyond belief. Eric himself summed it up nicely just this past holiday season. With a negative COVID test on his part, and two weeks of the strictest self-quarantining on my husband's and mine,

Eric drove from Tucson to San Diego in December for a visit. One evening while he cooked dinner, we got to chatting about our family and how fortunate the three of us are to relish spending time together—not a reality all families share.

"You know, Mom, it's like that saying that's been misinterpreted: blood is thicker than water. I think it's biblical, but I'm not sure," he said.

"Yeah, I don't know if it's biblical or not, though it's very familiar." I replied. "But what do you mean misinterpreted?"

"Well, I've heard that the original saying was: The blood of the covenant is thicker than the water of the womb. You know, like the tie with people we choose is stronger than with who we're related to simply by birth. The exact opposite of how we use it popularly."

"Wow," I uttered, stunned by yet another example of how human culture twisted what may have been divine insight for its own purposes of control.

"Yeah, really, but the cool thing is, with us, it's both."

"What do you mean, honey?" I asked.

"We're related, and that's a great bond, but I feel like we've made a covenant of caring, honesty, and support with one another that's even deeper," he said as he turned from washing vegetables in the sink and held my eyes in his loving gaze.

"We have, haven't we," I said, my heart swelling in gratitude for that very reality, for him, and for the healing journey that has made our depth of connection possible. Such unimaginable gifts. Trauma may be a family affair, but so is the possibility of post-traumatic growth, and we, the little Davidson clan, are living proof of that promise.

CHAPTER 9

Trauma: It's Also a National Affair

For a bit, I'm going to veer away from the solely personal—not that anything in this life can ever be solely personal, interconnected as we all are with each other and our world—because, just as the jump from seeing trauma in myself to seeing it in my family was easy, the jump to seeing it in my country wasn't difficult either. For starters, it seems clear that my experience of motherhood was made all the more traumatic because a social support system for mothers—typically, the primary caretakers of children—is essentially nonexistent here in the US, exacerbating the already undue stress put on parents and children by our isolationist model of the nuclear family. It's a tragic example of how we lack a system of true collective care, and I am sad and angry about this national reality.

But right now, just days following the brutal, senseless, ugly, shameful murder of George Floyd on May 25, 2020, overflowing with sorrow and vibrating with rage, I feel compelled, as if by forces beyond myself, to take a deep dive into a different example of this same national reality. What you will read here constitutes reckoning I did in years past, pre-COVID, interlaced with understanding I'm working out in this very moment, on this very page, as I write during the racial unrest swirling across our country and the globe. I'll try to give voice to what is rising in my heart and mind about how urgently important the discussion of trauma is for our nation.

The word *trauma* appears everywhere these days—on the news, on social media, on people's lips—and there is no more accurate word to describe the COVID pandemic itself and the multilayered upheaval accompanying it, especially the concurrent uprising against racism in the United States ignited by yet more instances of police brutality against Black Americans, including the slaying of Floyd. I couldn't be happier. Not about the alarming events and senseless tragedies causing us to utter the word *trauma*, of course. But about how it's *finally* being used to describe social, cultural, and systemic phenomena more loudly, more publicly, more in the mainstream—that is, the heretofore white-dominated world. Leaders from communities that are oppressed by our racialized society have been talking about the reality of metatrauma for ages, but because of that very oppression, their voices have been systematically marginalized, muted, even murdered. But no more.

In this crucible of time, we've reached a demographic and phenomenological tipping point. We've arrived at a collective place of no turning back, like when the personal constellation of crises forced my own hand back in 2016. The message in both cases—mine then, the nation's now—is the same: change or die. There is no way I could have kept going the way I was living my life, with my truth-denying pain-burying unconsciousness. I was headed for disaster—medical or otherwise. So, too, the United States. Our collective dark night of the soul has arrived, similarly both long overdue and pointing to the need for radical transformation.

I wish it didn't require catastrophe to bring about transformation. But it so often does, and it took coming to grips with my own experience of that story arc to recognize how it plays out in society too. It was also within my individual narrative that the deepest awakening to social injustice began for me. Without diving headlong into healing my own experiences of overwhelm, violation, and oppression and coming out the other side, I would not have developed the eyes to finally see what my non-white brothers and sisters have been so desperately crying out against for so long. I would not have cultivated the mind to understand the depth and implications of their suffering, nor the heart to hold both the pain and the hope I now have that humanity can find a way out of systemic oppression and a way forward into freedom and equity for all. For me, the universal started with the personal.

As I've shared throughout, the more I learned about and understood trauma for myself—how it had shaped my life—the more I saw its imprint and dynamic everywhere, including on the systemic levels of culture and society. Not surprising, I suppose, because culture and society are, after all, simply aggregate reflections of the human experience, institutions created by people—wounded people. Just as I grasped the fact that to heal my broken places and transform my life, I would have to face my pain, I realized that the same was true of our nation and its systems. Because I believe the work of social change always begins with the individual, I started by shining a spotlight on my own lack of consciousness as a member of the collective and began the education of Laurie about the problem of her racism.

Yes, *my* racism—I am a sixty-two-year-old product of the white supremacist system, and, just by virtue of my having grown up thus, racism is unavoidably in my makeup. I've not found it easy to grapple with this truth, but the effort—no matter how much discomfort it raises—is essential to my own growth and, more importantly, the healing of social injustice. James Baldwin said,

"Not everything that is faced can be changed, but nothing can be changed until it is faced." As I see it, *facing* means bringing into full consciousness, out of the shadows and into the light.

One of the trickiest obstacles to confronting my racism, discovered with the beam of my awareness, was shame. When I first sensed it, I don't know why it surprised me, because close examination quickly reveals obvious parallels between the organizing principles of the alcoholic family system I grew up in and the overarching white supremacist system. The most important parallel being that they are both shame based. Not in the life affirming, authentic shame that naturally flows within each person to guide our behavior toward personal and social good, but in an externalized, manufactured, inauthentic shame—an important difference insightfully described in Karla McLaren's book *The Language of Emotions*. In both toxic systems, in fact ubiquitously in our culture, this twisted tool of inauthentic shame is wielded with crippling effect as a means of control, as a way to perpetuate them—and any of the other harmful isms that characterize our world. I found myself in very familiar territory.

One of the tenets of white supremacy that keeps it locked in place is this: As a white person, you are either good, "not racist," or you are bad, "racist." As a means of perpetuating itself, it's a genius tactic, really, because who would ever voluntarily place themselves in the latter category, signing up for a hefty dose of externally induced shame? It incentivizes unconsciousness. The system clearly lies, though, doesn't it? From the healing work I've done around trauma, I've arrived at the hard-won place where I acknowledge my inborn essential value and that of *all* beings, so I reject the false dichotomy of good and bad people. I believe instead that behavior, not innate nature, is the real issue, and that it is ultimately about past history, fear levels, and degrees of wounding—for each and every one of us, individually and collectively.

Assuming I have understood him correctly, author, historian, antiracist scholar, and activist Ibram X. Kendi frames the issue most helpfully for me. He argues that it's actually impossible to be "not racist." A person is either actively behaving in an anti-racist manner—in thought, word, and deed—or in a racist manner. There is liberation in that assertion because it doesn't condemn my very being, locking me in inauthentic shame or freezing me into inaction. It allows me to meet with equanimity my fully complex human self as both a dreadfully flawed product of a horrific system and as a newly awakened, empowered agent for change. Secure in my innate value as a fellow member of *Homo sapiens*, I can claim my virtues and confront my sins, do the inner work to transcend the system of oppression I was raised in, and move forward in opposing it with my voice, my body, my dollars, my life.

It is essential for all white people in the US to wrestle with our transgressions. Without that inner reckoning, any statement made or action taken around racial justice will be polluted by unconsciousness, ineffective at best, but more likely harmfully upholding the very system that needs changing. I commenced my own wrestling in earnest a couple of years ago, first by reading *Biased* by social psychologist, author, and activist Jennifer L. Eberhardt and then *White Fragility* by author Robin DiAngelo. Each in her own way, a Black woman and a White woman, respectively, led me to begin to honestly look at my history, background, and current circumstances; to examine my hardwiring and defaults; and to confront the reality of my privilege and my failures to see and to act.

In reviewing my first twenty-odd years of life—in the 1960s and 1970s—which were spent in a 100 percent white small Connecticut town during the civil rights movement, I easily saw how my view of reality came to reflect elements of both the supremacist vision stitched into my rural-cum-suburban community and the call for equality transforming the wider world. By far the harder thing to look at was how my unconsciousness of the former persisted throughout my adulthood, despite sufficient opportunities to face the truth.

There were glimmers indicating I understood there was a better way, despite the specious programming I'd received and the segregated environments I'd inhabited as a child and teenager. As an undergraduate, I took courses in what was then known as the African American Studies Department at my college. I dated a Black man, off and on, throughout those years. Then in graduate school, I seized every opportunity to attend presentations by Black activist theologian Cornel West, who was a visiting faculty member, even though his courses were not part of my program. All these new behaviors seemed to mystify or, in a few cases, upset some of my white family and friends. I remember distinctly the disdain dripping from my father's voice when—referring to my first African American studies course—he asked me, "Whatever possessed you to take *that*?" Despite the subtle confusion or outright disapproval of those around me, though, I managed to stay open, curious, and concerned—at least part of me did. But I also remained stuck—a large part of me comfortable with the status quo, easy in my white structures, in my privilege to interact yet turn a blind eye to my personal culpability in maintaining racism or my responsibility for effecting change.

When I turned thirty-one and moved with my previous husband to the remote and lovely Taos, New Mexico, however, my comfort began to crumble. Taos is where I finally began to feel, on a somatic level, my inheritance of and participation in the white supremacist system; in this case, the atrocities my ancestors had perpetrated on Indigenous peoples and my lack of understanding and action. Upon first encountering the Tiwa Pueblo situated outside the main part of town, I had a profoundly visceral reaction: Awe at its quiet beauty and ancient solidity swelled in my chest, while sensations of grief choked my throat, and shame pulled at my gut. An experience of simultaneous ecstasy and agony, new to me, seemingly out of the blue, unsettling. I see now that my body was speaking, quite loudly; but at the time, I didn't yet know how to listen deeply.

When I resided there, the town's population was evenly divided among Hispanic, Indigenous, and white, a complex cultural environment unlike any I'd ever dwelt in before. It afforded me—really for the first time ever—direct exposure to the richness in differing lives, and I loved that opportunity, welcomed the learning and the broadening of my worldview. But with my head and heart still shut down tight against my own unprocessed trauma, I lacked the capacity to fully grasp the inequity and oppression—those ugly threads among the beautiful ones that I saw running through the three groups' fragile coexistence—to which this new environment also provided me direct exposure. Never mind the capacity to grasp my role in perpetuating them.

I became increasingly disheartened with living in Taos, unconsciously blaming my state on some surface externals of life there, and concluded I needed to leave. To justify my decision, I created a litany of reasons why it made sense—all related to personal comfort. The climate was too harsh, our housing too rustic, we were too far from a city. The irony here hits pretty hard, because now I understand that I likely fled Taos, after only a year and a half, to avoid feeling uncomfortable on a much deeper plane, probably exhausted by the effort to keep from seeing and dealing with painful inner and outer realities. And where did I go? Boulder, Colorado. Back to the kind of community I was used to—very white—to a place where I could try and pretend all was right with the world.

It's funny how life finds us, though, isn't it? Fast forward only a few years, and I'd divorced, remarried, and, together with my second husband and our two-and-a-half-year-old son, had moved to San Diego. I now found myself back in a multicultural community, and my family had expanded to include Rick's uncle and his wife, Althea, a woman of color. The realities of daily living among much greater human diversity, together with the opportunity to get to know Althea intimately, hear her stories of pain and oppression, and watch her make choices about where she lived and with whom she socialized, challenged much of my experience and many of my assumptions. My blinders started to come off for good.

The final push for my wake-up call came when I took a job at a community college and for the first time in my life, worked for an institution that was not predominantly white. Not only was the student body incredibly diverse, but so were the faculty, staff, and executive leadership. The six years I worked there brought great learning, especially around privilege. My job as a grant writer for the money-raising arm of the college required me to listen deeply to various people—professors, administrators, counselors—so that I could capture their visions, requirements, and plans in the written word. All these folks worked on the front lines, serving students—most of whom were from minority populations—who needed extra support to succeed: first generation college goers, former foster youth, veterans, the homeless, and the food-challenged.

The raw stories of disadvantage, discrimination, and deprivation I heard stunned me, painting vivid pictures of lives lived so very differently than mine and for no reason other than circumstances of birth. I also soaked up many inspiring stories of triumph, perseverance, and success, despite seemingly insurmountable obstacles. Slowly and steadily, layers of delusion about my own agency in the educational, economic, and other advantages of my life began to fall away. Even so, I'm sorry to say that, in my case, old patterns die hard, and I remember with great regret a conflict I had with a

Latina colleague that arose shortly before I left that job during our collaboration on a grant application for a program she was running.

Our work together started off well. I sat in Ynez's office, mesmerized by her passion and eloquence as she described her important mission and the students and community members it served, and I felt hopeful that together we'd be able to capture her vision and land the money she needed. Because of tight timing and the large number of projects I already had on deadline, the plan we came up with was that she would write the first draft of the grant narrative, and I would provide editing services and take care of the technicalities of submission.

Just as I recall how impressed I was with Ynez's ability to paint a picture with her spoken words, to tell a compelling story while we talked, I also remember how stunned I was by her written words, but not in a good way. Her first draft was devoid of her lovely animating spirit; her words, to me, fell flat. I couldn't find any pictures painted in them to stir a grantor's heart. In addition, her effort was flawed grammatically, structurally, and compositionally, requiring attention beyond the mere edit I had time for. As I saw it then, we had problems, and they stemmed from her writing. So, I reached out to Ynez to talk about the situation in what, I deludedly thought, was a diplomatic manner.

I wish I could sit down with Ynez now and apologize for my offense those many years ago, for my blindness and ignorance and the difficulties they raised between us, for the pain I caused her. We did indeed have problems, but they had nothing to do with her writing. We had the problem of my unconsciousness of my white privilege and my insensitivity to English being her second language, not to mention the whole twisted world of grants. I was blithely participating in a system where power and money—most often gained, in the first place, on the backs of people disadvantaged and oppressed by the white supremacist system—are concentrated in the hands of a very select few whites, who then turn around and deign to "give" it to those very same people. Making them jump through hoops to get it—beg, essentially. All the while insisting that their applications conform to exacting language standards inculcated by the same system that has kept them down and often excluded them from the educational opportunity to learn those very standards. We had problems all right—so obvious to me now, but still beyond my grasp then. I even reacted self-protectively with denial when, in discussing the conflict that arose between Ynez and me, my supervisor appropriately raised the issue of my racism.

It wasn't until I started my own personal healing journey in earnest that I could finally see my defensiveness clearly and begin the work of dropping it. Cultivating mindful self-compassion proved key to enabling that shift. No longer so afraid of what I might find when I looked inside myself, more comfortable with reality in its complex fullness, and surer in my inherent worth no matter what, I was able to uncover the layers, patterns, and habits of my own racism, offer acceptance, and affirm the need for transformation. Now, I try to practice greeting any new arising of it with some version of, "Okay. Here it still is. A chance to grow further." Then I do more of the inner work required to abolish it, along with the outer work required to make amends for it.

While I may have transcended denial that bias is there, I have watched myself sometimes swing too wildly in the other direction, automatically and harshly condemning myself for the racism behind my behavior in a particular situation when it may not actually be there. A different kind of reflex than denial, but also unfortunate and unskillful in its unconsciousness. A "self-flagellation for a self-perceived offense," as a woman of color I know astutely called it, that helps no one. Sometimes shades of gray permeate an interaction, and dancing with nuance is required. So, I'm learning to pause, to get present, and to ask myself *how* and *why* my thoughts and actions might be reflective of ingrained white supremacy, to look carefully. Because, as that same woman helped me see, open and honest dialogue with ourselves about things we might not be seeing—in essence, an aware responsiveness, not emotional reactivity—is really where the consideration of implicit bias bears fruit for us all.

It's a sobering reckoning to confront one's own participation in the oppression of other people, but I highly recommend getting sober in this arena (actually, in all arenas), though it's not for the faint of heart. During recovery from alcoholism, an addict must tackle the host of unsettling feelings and memories that made them want to drink as a way to escape in the first place. Similarly, in looking at my history in the arena of racial action—or inaction as was more the case—I have confronted my own ignorance, apathy, fear, insensitivity, guilt, cowardice, shame, and more. As with recovery, on the other side of all this unsightliness, I am finding clearer vision and a sense of my ability and responsibility to make changes and different choices. I know my work of examination and repair is far from over. In fact, I suspect it will go on for the rest of my life as I expose deeper layers of hidden programming, grow into greater wholeness, and develop more courage and stamina for the work of justice—echoes of the trajectory of my own comeback from trauma.

On a personal level, I learned that to heal I had to get real, and the same goes for the collective. Because the science of trauma tells us that wounds laid down in relationship can only be mended in relationship, it's imperative that everyone tackle curing racial injustice. The work will necessarily look different for various individuals and groups of people, but it's one united effort, and it's about growth and wholeness for all. Murri artist, activist, and academic Lilla Watson, voicing the sentiment of many Australian Indigenous people, is quoted as saying it this way: "If you have come here to help me, you are wasting your time. But if you have come because your liberation is bound up with mine, then let us work together." As I see it, it's really the same process. My healing—and yours—*is* the culture's, and vice versa; and it's ultimately all about trauma.

I'm reminded of Gabor Maté's succinct description of personal trauma as separation—from one's own gut feelings, instincts, authentic emotions, in essence from the truth of oneself. Well, the United States as a nation was born predicated on that very thing, on separation— from the truth that we are one human family. Yes, differences in physical characteristics exist. For example, humans inhabit infinitely various places on the *Homo sapiens* grayscale, and diversity needs to be honored and celebrated, but erroneous concepts like "race" and "whiteness" are completely fabricated. These fundamental untruths of separateness at the very root of white supremacy were a convenient and potent means of asserting control, maintaining power, and ensuring massive economic gain for a few, right from the start of our country. They are now maintained—in the face of overwhelming scientific proof of their falsehood—out of fear and stubbornness, to the peril of all, even those they initially "protected." As does any such strategy, our system of oppression wounds us all. Not to the same degree, of course, but it hurts and harms *everyone*.

Ranking trauma is rightfully perceived as a dangerous undertaking fraught with traps, but I find myself wondering who may have suffered the most from the twisted way we have historically organized ourselves as a society. It may not be a question that can be answered definitively, or even should be asked; however, my musings on the subject led me to this: it's not simply white supremacy that holds our nation in thrall. It's white, male, heterosexual, cisgender, able-bodied—you name the "norm"— supremacy. So, while I listen to and learn from all voices of color on this journey toward healing racial injustice, I have purposely sought out the wisdom of those consigned to the bottom of the too-long-enduring, fallacious, and poisonous hierarchy that has shaped our culture. In paying the highest price, perhaps they have the most to teach. My search has led me to people of color who self-identify as women or LGBTQIA+, like adrienne maree brown, Sherri Taylor, Layla Saad, Joi Lewis, Tiffany Jana, and Rhonda V. Magee—all important leaders on the frontlines of the movement for liberation, equality, and justice.

Some of these folks—as well as others, including Resmaa Menakem—are courageously applying a somatic understanding of trauma to the issue of racism in our country. This heartens me because that lens focuses the light of truth exactly where it belongs: on the body. For over four centuries, we have perpetrated appalling physical, emotional, mental, and spiritual harm on one another, and it has inevitably manifested in personal bodies as profound levels of individual disease, and in the collective body as rampant social ills—inescapable realities confronting us no matter where we look today. As I came to know in my own life and have stated before in these pages, trauma is life threatening, and the effects are cumulative over the generations.

When I pause, breathe deeply, and really absorb what that last clause I wrote means specifically for Black and Indigenous people in the United States—a nation founded on the twin evils of slavery and genocide—I shudder. In addition to the harm that they unavoidably endure in this lifetime because of entrenched biases and structures of oppression, their bodies harbor the toxic, undischarged energy of four hundred years of unspeakable atrocities. I know from lived experience what it feels like to pay the price of chronic traumatic stress—to exist trapped in its painful, devastating, potentially lethal consequences. Yet what I have carried in my lifetime—including my ancestral load—is infinitesimal in scope and scale compared to what my Black and Indigenous brothers and sisters bear on personal, intergenerational, and sociocultural levels.

The implications of this truth seem almost too enormous to grasp or process, but that is what I believe I'm called to do as a citizen of this country—to face the collective grief and shame of its harrowing history, because it is real. My blood boils, and then I move into deep sadness, when people claim that my view is unpatriotic. My response is, "If truth telling is unpatriotic, then so be it." They've missed the point anyway. It's time we Americans wiped the concept of patriotism from our list of cherished values. (After all, it comes from the Latin root *pater*, meaning "father." Need I say more?) Instead, I propose using "Love for One Another" as our guiding principle. Cornel West nailed it when he said, "Never forget that justice is what love looks like in public."

I had an odd experience years ago directly related to West's assertion, but I didn't know it at the time. It was winter 1992, I had been dating Rick for a few months, and we were headed to meet friends of his for a weekend of skiing in Steamboat Springs, Colorado. A long drive afforded us the luxury of hours to talk, to get to know one another more thoroughly, and revel in that glorious new relationship excitement at deepening intimacy. During a natural lull in the conversation, I gazed out the window at the stunning mountain scenery we were traversing and must have passed into a state of reverie. Suddenly, a phrase came to me, silently yet thunderously, "My purpose in life is to embody love." I sat up, shook my head, and looked around me, glancing over at Rick who was driving—I guess to see if he had heard anything. Clearly, he hadn't. Not as familiar then—nor as comfortable—as I am now with these kinds of spiritual downloads, I held the experience close to my chest at the time, not telling Rick about my "message from God," if you will, for quite a while. But it stayed with me vividly, and over the years, I quietly worked with the phrase, kind of as my guiding principle.

The problem, and why I bring up this experience now, though it may seem unrelated to a discussion of racism, is that I unfortunately did just what Dr. West bade me not to. In interpreting the call I received to embody love as having meaning only in my private realm—as about how I needed to treat myself, be in a couple with Rick, raise a family—I neglected love in the public sphere. I forgot justice. Now, however, thanks to trauma recovery, I've remembered, and I'm committed to embodying love in *all* areas of my life—with my whole being—including as a citizen of the United States.

So far, what that looks like for me is: continuing to work on surfacing and examining my own biases; initiating conversations with other white individuals about our responsibility to prioritize the fight for justice for all; speaking up when I encounter racist behavior in others, and staying open when others point it out in me; voting very carefully at the polls and with my day-to-day spending in support of equity; and divesting all financial holdings in companies that in any way perpetuate the system of oppression while looking for opportunities to invest in and support minority-owned businesses; among other ways. I know it's just a beginning, the early stages of fleshing out what love in action on the national scale means for me. I'm not sure what it will look like in the future as I learn and grow. As with the rest of this surprising heroine's journey I've been on, I have a hunch it will take me to unexpected places, and I hope to meet you along the way. Let's practice very public love together.

CHAPTER 10

Redeeming the Reverend

I'm starting this chapter where I left off in the last one, with love. The whole question of life boils down to this one thing. Love is as real as it gets, and I've known this truth for a long time, not just intellectually but also on a much more fundamental, energetic level of understanding—long before I received that direct message on the road to Steamboat Springs. Perhaps I was born knowing it. Maybe we all are. And the real tragedy of trauma is that it disconnects us from the totality of that consciousness. It must not wipe it away altogether, though, or we wouldn't have survived as a species. In fact, I have a hunch it was a remnant of this inner wisdom about love—the light at my core—that was the spark that twice kept me from ending my own life. In any case, I can gaze back over my years and find numerous places where I attempted to reconnect with love as my ground and to live my life in alignment with it. Some of those efforts proved more successful than others, but all were parts of a journey home to the essence of my being.

One of the most significant of these endeavors transpired when I answered what I experienced then as a call to the ministry. True confessions time: I was ordained as a Christian pastor back in 1986. So, just call me Reverend. No, actually, please don't. When I left the church only three short years after it had been bestowed, I sought to formally renounce my ordination, but the powers that be would hear none of it. Apparently, once a reverend always a reverend. So, to this day, I bear the title, though I don't identify with it or use it. Every once in a while, a black-and-white reminder arrives in my mailbox in the form of a letter from the pension fund addressed to Reverend Laurie Lee Davidson. It's a hoot each time—seeing it written—coming face-to-face with who I was in a past life, who I am now, and the blessings in the transformation.

That metamorphosis took a long time—some thirty years—completing in the fall of 2019 in a most unlikely place. Strangely enough, I found closure around my painful pastoral tenure on the dance floor. I began consistently attending 5Rhythms classes in January of 2019 and was surprised at how quickly the regular gathering became important to me. It formed a touchstone, a weekly ritual that brought joy, healing, and meaning to my life. I eagerly looked forward to it during the other six days, and the fact that class met on Sunday mornings, in a powerful echo of my previous devotional life, amused me. About a month after I started, a substitute leader stepped in for one session. Our usual teacher was out of town and had arranged for Jenelle Smith, a teacher-in-training—a Space-Holder in 5R lingo —to cover for her.

I'm not sure why, but I connected strongly with Jenelle's music choices. One of the richest things about 5R is that each facilitator brings their unique self to bear on the experience, so no two classes are the same, and I love that diversity. It broadens and enriches me. Anyway, I was especially absorbed in her offering that day, fully inhabiting my body and moving lots of energy and emotion up and through in synch with the music. In the concluding rhythm of *stillness*, at the end of the second Wave we danced, the haunting melody and lyrics of the last song—in a language I didn't recognize—drew me down to the floor in supplication. By the end, I lay on my back with my hands over my heart, feeling a profound fullness, a deep sense of connection to something huge, a force beyond me. I listened to the fading bars of unearthly notes with tears, of what I wasn't sure—joy? sadness?—leaking out from between my closed eyelids, as I caught the final word, a familiar *amen*.

I had been moved by songs in 5R before, but this one had brought me to another level all together, so after class, I introduced myself to Jenelle and inquired about that last piece of music. Turns out it came from Lisa Gerrard and Patrick Cassidy's album *Immortal Memory* and was entitled "Abwoon," its lyrics the Lord's Prayer in Jesus's original language of Aramaic. Upon hearing this, goose bumps rose all over my body, the words "Oh, my God" burst out of me, and I felt a simultaneous anchoring to the earth and uprising of my spirit. It was a powerful moment, in which I understood that 5R was how I worship, how I honor Divine Love with my body and soul, and I suddenly saw my church phase in a new light. I realized that back then, during my stint in the ministry, I had just been "looking for love in all the wrong places."

Before I left the dance studio that day, I ascertained from Jenelle that she held her own regular weekly 5R sessions about an hour away from where I live. Much to my surprise, I also learned that her Wednesday night offerings—Sweats in 5R lingo, after founder Gabrielle Roth's encouragement to "sweat your prayers" on the dance floor—were held in a church. I sensed immediately that I had to go. I wasn't sure precisely why, just that I felt an urgent desire to dance in that place, and soon. However, like the gap between when I realized I needed to take Mindful Self-Compassion and when I actually enrolled in it, a few months went by before I made the excursion. I suspect the delay was again about integration. I needed to inhabit and process more deeply the amazing experience I'd just had so that I could be fully resourced and present to the one to come.

When I did embark on it, I treated my trip to her class as a sacred pilgrimage. I took the afternoon off and explored the community where it was held since I'd never been there before. I didn't set an agenda beyond spending some of my time on the beach and grabbing an early dinner to give my body plenty of fuel—and time to digest it—before an hour and a half of vigorous dancing. While I remained essentially planless, before setting out I meditated with the intention of grounding myself in an attitude of presence, trust in emergence, and openness to flow. In the light of that strong intention, the day unfolded effortlessly and delightfully.

It started with two obvious miracles for anyone familiar with life in coastal Southern California: a traffic-free drive and a perfect parking spot just waiting for me, right in the center of town, only steps from the beach. Then, while poking around, grabbing a meal, or having a moment of rest, I had the most extraordinary encounters with perfect strangers. Like the multigenerational members of the Martinez family who ran the restaurant I drifted into at 3:00 p.m. to have my oddly early dinner. They welcomed me heartily—a woman alone—and made me feel like I was joining them for shared sustenance in their own home. Or like the woman, maybe around the same age as I, it was hard to tell, who sat down at the other end of the park bench I'd perched on with a book after dinner. She softly asked me what I was reading, launching us into unexpectedly deep sharing about our lives, a conversation I reluctantly had to end to get to my 5R class on time. We talked openly like old friends, though we never even exchanged names. With gifts like these encounters peppering my explorations, the whole time in town felt magical, and I reached the church that evening primed for a powerful experience, which is exactly what I got.

When I'd looked up the address before setting off on my trip, I'd discovered that it wasn't just any old church hosting the 5R session. It was the exact denomination I had served as a minister long ago. I would be "returning to the scene of the crime," and I wondered if I might feel some discomfort at such a direct reminder of those difficult years. As I put one foot in front of the other and climbed the hill leading from the parking lot to the front of the building, I felt keenly aware of my surroundings. It was right around sunset, and the light inhabited that enchanting liminal place between day and night. A few blocks from the shore, the air smelled less strongly of the sea and was overlaid by the warm scent of honeysuckle from a vine twining up a fence along the path. Birds sang their quieting down evening songs. My senses took all of this in, and at the same time, I stood outside myself, witnessing my own alertness. When I rounded the corner and came face-to-face with a sign naming the church and proclaiming its denomination, I gasped. Not in pain, as I'd anticipated, but in joy. I felt a sweetness and a solace—a homecoming—that swept me right in the door.

The hall where the dance took place that night was this church's first official sanctuary now turned all-purpose gathering space and was stunningly lovely with a soaring arched ceiling, enormous, mullioned windows, and an exquisite honey-hued oak floor. Every 5R class space, no matter where it is set up, includes a multimedia art installation. It's an altar of sorts, often created by a student, sometimes together with the teacher. The one this night reflected the fall equinox, which fast approached. Echoing that theme as the music began, Jenelle invited us to consider the meaning of the seasons and passages in our lives, and I thought to myself, *Could that suggestion be any more on-point for me?*

Oh, my goodness, I danced my heart out that night, and it was purely and utterly redeeming, in *all* the senses of that word: to get or win back; to help to overcome something detrimental; to release from blame or debt; to clear; to change for the better; to reform, repair, restore; to offset the bad effect of. When it was all done, I rejoiced at having danced in church—expressing my truest self, connecting with the divine—and at having my offering well and truly accepted. I left in a state of peaceful euphoria, grateful for the precious gift I'd been given, and drove home feeling so clean and clear and loved. Loved not just by Jenelle and the other people who had readily shared themselves with me on the dance floor, in the circle afterward, and in conversation as we were departing, but also by the whole experience. Strangely, even by the space itself.

When I later got curious and read about the church I'd just danced in, it made perfect sense to me why I might have felt that way. The congregation takes seriously the effort to embody Christ's message of love for all by practicing radical inclusivity, prioritizing social justice, and even going beyond the boundaries of their own religion. In addition to being guided by the teachings of Jesus, their online self-description declared them to be open to learning and drawing from the richness of other faith traditions, embracing of all spiritual paths and all people who seek to know God, a sanctuary for individual and communal spiritual growth, and committed to transforming the world. The night I danced there, I had absorbed this accepting, embracive, global vibe—a very different one than was present in the two churches I had served three decades past and a whole continent's breadth away.

I couldn't help but wonder how my life story might have unfolded differently if those earlier congregations had resembled this one, if they had been more open, more about embodying unity and compassion. But then I reminded myself that during that long-ago period in my life, I was still stuck in trauma aftermath. I remained out of touch with my love-based core, so of course my outer reality necessarily reflected that inner state of alienation. Also, though it was very painful at the time, my conflict with the church played an important part in my ultimate liberation, so I'm grateful for the experience—all of it, the good and the ill. A brief glimpse at my tumultuous time as a pastor will reveal why my dancing in this particular church many years later was so redemptive, why the congregation's courageous vision and my healing journey were bound to cohere.

During the time I served in the Christian ministry, my understanding of Jesus's message about God, love, and the life of the Spirit evolved beyond the tenets of the church as humans have created it, which was an unsettling thing to have happen to someone vowed to uphold those tenets. But there I was. The more I studied Jesus's words, took them into my being, and committed to living them out, the more I understood how terribly wrong I'd gotten it.

It became crystal clear to me that his message called each of us to recognize our own divinity, as reflections of the Source, and to treat each other with love in light of that powerful truth. He had been urging individuals to claim for themselves and each other the holy "I Am," not to bestow it on some anointed other. I grew increasingly uncomfortable with the trappings of my "ordained" position—with standing up on altars elevated above the congregation, with wearing a special robe, with bearing a title of distinction, with acting as intermediary—when it seemed to me that Jesus himself taught that access to the divine is direct, for everyone. My whole being cried out that he would be horrified to see the hierarchy that we'd created in his name.

This transformation didn't occur in a vacuum. It developed within the context of my initial awakening to trauma—though no one was naming it that yet—which began after I entered divinity school. A year into the three-year degree program, I began to struggle in my first marriage and sought therapy for the first time. While I found the process only moderately helpful, it did plant an important seed for the future. As I was leaving his office at the conclusion of our final session, that first counselor said, "You know, at some point, you're going to have to look deeply at your mother's drinking and how it affected you." That point came a couple of years later when I took my second job as an ordained pastor, and my new circumstances brought me into more sustained contact with my parents than I'd had in years. I couldn't sidestep the pain any longer. So, I sought out a counselor who specialized in adult children of alcoholics (ACOA), and she helped me begin to purge the emotional and relational toxins I'd absorbed in my upbringing. I can't overstate the significance of this work and how it helped me make sense of my concurrent struggles in the ministry.

As I engaged in my personal healing, I soon recognized unmistakable parallels between the alcoholic family system and the church system I found myself in. Let me be quick to state that I did not arrive at this assessment through mere casual observation or philosophical musings. I arrived at it through the suffering—personal and professional—that I encountered as a woman trying to participate fully in leadership in a two-thousand-year-old entrenched patriarchy. The discrimination began almost immediately upon graduation, when I applied for my first associate pastor position out of school and was passed over for someone "more qualified." One of my mentors—who cared not about gender and was probably the only man within the church hierarchy ever truly to champion me—had an in with that congregation's search committee and informed me that the reason they'd given me for their decision was patently false, simply code for "male." While I found this fact hurtful, I bounced back—labeling it an anomaly—and accepted a different position with an open heart.

The senior pastor at this other church was considerably more casual and welcoming than the other had been and, during the hiring process, treated me in a respectful yet affable manner. So, when I entered his office on the very first day of the job, for our inaugural staff meeting, I felt hopeful.

"Welcome, Laurie! Please, come in and sit down. Make yourself comfortable," Adam said with a smile, gesturing to one of two chairs that formed a kind of sitting area in a corner of the room.

"Thanks, Adam," I replied as I settled myself in, familiar new-adventure butterflies flitting about my stomach.

"I hope you've got what you need in your office. If we've forgotten anything, just let me know, and I'll see that you get it," he asserted while he took the seat opposite me.

"I will, definitely. So far, I seem to have everything," I replied warmly, appreciating his consideration.

"So," he said, leaning forward in his chair, placing his forearms on his thighs, and clasping his hands together, dark eyes searching mine. "I have to tell you; I am attracted to you. Of course, we're both married, and it can't go anywhere, but I thought it was important to put it out there right away."

If I had been the mindful and healing woman back then that I am today, I would have been able to pause, sense into the anger naturally arising within me at the violation of collegial boundaries, and respond calmly and appropriately from a place of personal power to what clearly constituted sexual harassment. But I wasn't. At that point, I was a still-frozen trauma victim—all too familiar with and tragically accepting of this kind of dynamic, and many years would pass before I would awaken to the full import of its wrongness. Instead, I immediately went numb and mumbled something like, "Well, thank you for telling me." And the two years I served that parish remained clouded over with disquiet, awkwardness, and fear that all went unnamed.

Adam wasn't the only one to say things like that to me over my tenure as a pastor. A male parishioner once spent several minutes during the coffee hour following a Sunday service that I'd led, regaling me with his experience of gazing at my "shapely black-stocking-clad ankles alluringly taunting me from beneath your robe." I kid you not. Now, if men's struggles had stopped at my appearance, it would have been bad enough, but they went beyond it to who I was as a person, as a woman, to the feminine energy that I naturally brought to my work.

In fact, the head pastor of another church I served—the very person who originally suggested to me that I might have a calling in the ministry and who encouraged me throughout my studies and first pastorate—fiercely opposed me at every turn when we actually began to work together on the same staff. Seems I brought a different kind of energy to the role of minister—softer and more directly approachable than his. Not better, just different. But instead of welcoming the balance, seeking not only to teach and mentor but also to learn and grow himself—as I now know healthy leaders do—he appeared to struggle with the parishioners' hearty welcome of me and fell into a habit of almost constant criticism of my approach, disapproval of my ideas, and at times backhanded undermining of my credibility.

So, you see, the core message I repeatedly received—in both subtle and blatant ways, particularly from men above me on the ladder of authority—was the same one I had received in my family of origin: you are different, and that is bad; we do not want you here. Realizing I had been drawn to the church because of the familiarity of that message, because it confirmed my inner picture of unworthiness, jolted me awake. However, even though my ACOA therapy had helped me see that my personal growth toward wholeness demanded I leave the institution, it was not an easy awareness to embrace. Nothing is black or white; it's all shades of gray, right? I'd invested considerable time, energy, and money along the way to pastoring and loved much about the church—the holy music, the communion with other souls, the quiet contemplation, the commitment to help those in need. Plus, despite the difficulties within the hierarchy, most congregants had welcomed me with open arms, supported me, and rooted for me to continue.

But the path I needed to take for my own well-being appeared clear, and even though it led me out the narthex door and into the unknown, I stepped onto it, and I'm so glad I did. By leaving the church—a very public act—I made my first outward commitment to my changing inner reality, to liberating myself from old inherited programming of unworthiness. I'm grateful that, thirty years later, this path took me to a sister church dedicated to a completely different message: you are welcome just as you are; we love you. It reflected back to me my transformed sense of self. At this point in my journey, I don't feel drawn to return to Christianity or any organized religion, but I rejoice that there is at least one congregation out there daring to be so radical. After all, Jesus's original message was just that.

And so, I circle back to the song "Abwoon"—his words put to music—through which I was led to dance in a church and reclaim the fullness of my spirituality. The *Abwoon d'bwashmaya* is the Lord's Prayer (or the Our Father, as it's variously referred to in Christianity) in the original Aramaic. It is astonishingly beautiful, and, as I discovered, its translation to English bears little or no resemblance to the prayer promulgated by the church. Since the nuances, subtleties, and complexities of the ancient Aramaic language are layered and rich, I'm indebted to the tireless scholars who opened its treasures to me. Imagine my delight in discovering that Jesus's references to the source of creation were not gender specific, his vision of the divine was both personal and transpersonal, his concept of Spirit was grounded in the literal breath, and his image of heaven was not of something metaphysical but of the very Universe that we inhabit. Like the true mystic activist he was, he invoked embodiment as transcendence—a concept I deeply resonate with.

So, it appears the foundational prayer of the Christian faith is probably not the one that Christ himself uttered, but that doesn't surprise me. His message was too extreme for the times he inhabited. (Perhaps for any time?) Like many prophets, he cried out for total transformation, not just personal but structural as well—in the realms of politics, socioeconomics, culture, and religion. Unfortunately, what happened in response to his revolutionary call constituted only a minor adjustment. The Christian church that grew up in the wake of his life represents just a slight repackaging of the preexisting dynamic of separation; simply a different cloaking of a fear-based worldview with its othering and self-sanctioned behaviors of exclusion, oppression, and worse, which run completely counter to the love that Jesus cried out for people to live from.

The vast amount of hate spewed across our world right now, in the early days of January 2021, reflects how many people still operate from this fear-based worldview—frozen in survival mode, disconnected by inherited trauma from the truth of their intrinsic worthiness and unity with all beings. The members of the attempted government coup here in the United States are vivid examples. To echo the title of Gerald Jampolsky's brilliant book *Love Is Letting Go of Fear*, it is my fiercest hope that, by growing individually and collectively in capacity and commitment to embody love of self and other in our diversity and our oneness, we can thaw the icy grip of manufactured fear. Once the free-flowing usefulness of natural fear is restored to its rightful place alongside all human emotions—for there are real and important things to be afraid of, though "the other" is not one of them—its stuck version might no longer dominate our literal and figurative landscape, opening greater possibilities for communal healing. Now more than ever, a radical shift in consciousness is required—a shift into Love—and, this time, it's not just a single prophet urging us to change. It's many voices, even planet Earth herself, screaming out the challenge. I hope we answer the call. I'm trying to. How about you?

CHAPTER 11

Love Closer to Home

This is a good time to share more deeply one of the most profound ripple effects rendered by my personal metamorphosis. In chapter 3, I stated that, because of my healing journey, I now enjoy a deeper, more honest, and more mutually supportive bond with my husband. While that's indeed true (I wouldn't have claimed it otherwise), I don't want to give the impression that our marriage went unscathed in the process. In fact, we periodically entertain the possibility of its ending. It may be difficult to understand how those seemingly opposite statements can hold together—we have a loving relationship; we may split up—so I'll endeavor to explain.

At the core of this seeming paradox lies my understanding of love. As I've come to know it, love is not an emotion. It's a state of being from which behaviors spring. One that I'm learning to inhabit more and more as my growth toward wholeness progresses. Many years ago, when I read M. Scott Peck's *The Road Less Traveled*, I was struck by his portrayal of love as the will to exert oneself for the spiritual growth of another, or for one's own growth when talking about self-love. That way of conceptualizing it spoke to me, especially because his idea of "spiritual" seemed so broad—about the whole person. It still speaks to me, but I also believe that love is ultimately ineffable. I could spend hours chasing the words to express what I understand it to be and never capture its essence. For me, love transcends language, but I know what it feels like in my body.

Perhaps it's no surprise that I've come back to the body. After all, trauma recovery taught me that it's pretty much where everything in my life begins and ends, *the* place where I experience this fleeting human existence. So, of course, love abides here too. When I'm in touch with it, I sense my whole being infused with a shining tranquil pulsation: my heart feels full, my mind spacious, my chest light, my belly buoyant, my energy vibrant. It's a total body experience like no other. Unearthing this feeling from deep within me and relearning its instantiation and outward expression—the crucial tasks of these last few years—caused seismic shifts in me as a person. How could that movement not have affected my relationship with Rick?

After my defining moment, when I purposefully started to tune into myself, I had to confront how unhappy I felt in my marriage. Even though I was part of a stable couple and everything appeared fine by most cultural measures, I carried a deep sense of loneliness, feeling painfully disconnected from the person I lived in close quarters with. Each night during the early phase of my awakening, I'd take my bleeding heart to bed, only for the protective scab that formed overnight to get ripped off anew in the face of words said or unsaid, actions taken or untaken the next day. Such as when, shortly after realizing I bore the unprocessed energy of rape in my body, I decided I needed to share some of this understanding with Rick. This was raw stuff, and I felt nervous when I asked him one Saturday afternoon, "Could we talk about some of what's coming up for me in therapy?"

"Of course," he replied, and we moved to sit side-by-side on the living room couch.

"It's about rape and sexual violence," I ventured, wanting to prepare him for what was to come. He was aware that I was a survivor, but we had never really delved deeply into my story—because *I* hadn't.

"Okay, tell me," he responded quietly, giving me his full attention.

I took a deep breath and began. I don't remember the words I used, but I do recall the torrential flood of memory and emotion, the pain and anguish, that rushed out with them. As I struggled to recount past incidents of sexual abuse and tried to express what I was learning about their significance for my present, tears streamed down my face, sobs convulsed me, and snot flowed freely from my nose. It was a powerful "ugly cry" that almost overwhelmed me. When the wave of emotion finally passed, and I settled, there was a brief pause before Rick spoke.

"Don't you think the vast majority of women have had similar experiences to the ones you described?" he asked.

I sat up, stiffened, and pulled away from him, mumbling something like, "Yeah, probably," only vaguely aware of my own disquiet. A conversation lasting for only a few minutes ensued about the tragic ubiquity of sexual violence against women, and then he went his way, and I went mine. Later in the day, when I had some time to myself in which to reflect, I got in touch with how very unheard, uncared for, and alone I felt, and how absolutely typical of us our exchange had been. It was an old familiar pattern: me getting lost in my emotions, he staying in his head, neither of us getting what we really needed. In addition to feeling angry at him and sad for myself, I also felt confused and scared about our future. Nothing between *us* had changed, but apparently, *I* was changing. I was no longer blind to or okay with our unsatisfying interaction, and I wondered if I could go on—if I *should* go on—with the marriage.

This awareness of my uneasiness cut like a double-edged sword. Some moments, I just wanted to go back to sleep, return to not seeing what was wrong, to not feeling the pain. I'd ask myself, *Isn't what we have good enough? Who am I to be unhappy with this perfectly fine man, with the comfortable life we've built?* Once begun, though, there's no turning back on the road to consciousness, because, as Oliver Wendell Holmes so beautifully put it, "A mind that is stretched by a new experience can never go back to its old dimensions." I had to accept that it was impossible for me to unlearn the new ways of being I was cultivating, even if I wanted to. And frankly, I didn't want to. Because, despite what looked to me like the impending doom of my marriage, I was feeling more alive, more whole, more like what I'd begun to identify as my true self than ever before. And surely, that was a good thing. Wasn't it? The only viable way forward, as I saw it, was to continue my quest for well-being and see where it led me, led us.

I plowed on. Throughout Mindfulness-Based Stress Reduction, Mindful Self-Compassion, and my somatic therapy, throughout the whole damn odyssey, I kept a lot of my inner experience to myself—having learned the hard way through our rape conversation debacle that oversharing was not helpful to either of us, that I could not expect Rick to be like my therapist. Instead, I painted for Rick the broad strokes of what I was learning and going through, the struggles and the triumphs. While he sometimes appeared to me confused and troubled by my pain and difficulties, I constantly felt his unselfish support of my healing process—even as I raised the specter of my doubts about our marriage. Having accompanied me through some of the darkest points of my life, he expressed genuine delight in my personal growth, in my development before his eyes into a more stable, healthy, powerful woman.

I quail at the confession I'm about to make, but initially, I actually tried to pin all my problems with our relationship on Rick.

Inanities like "If only *he* were different, then *I* would be happy," ran rampant in my brain. I ruminated obsessively on his "flaws": emotionally stunted, relationally defensive, unable to connect deeply. Thankfully, my therapist gently but relentlessly brought me back to myself, to what my feelings and thoughts about Rick meant about me, to how I was often projecting onto him my own inner reality. She was dogged in this effort, and, at first, I felt infuriated by her persistence. After a while, I welcomed it, sometimes even beating her to the punch by saying, "I know. How does this reflect back on me, right?" and laughing in celebration at how quickly I began to catch myself.

Slowly but surely, I was discovering how old wounds, inaccurate understandings, and erroneous assumptions—my unconscious patterns—stemming from my traumatic early years had polluted my perceptions of myself, Rick, and our marriage. I realized that much of what I felt, experienced, and thought about my present reality didn't belong there but to the past. One day, perhaps a year into therapy, bearing a lot of pain from some interaction with Rick—the specific content of which I can't even remember now—I dragged myself into Gloria's office, plopped down on the couch with a sigh, and declared, "I'm done!"

"With what?" she asked quietly.

"With my marriage," I shakily replied. "I can't take the loneliness and alienation anymore."

"Hmm," she murmured and paused briefly, holding me in her loving and level gaze. "While you may well choose at some point in the future to end your marriage, for right now, let's see if we can figure out what it is that you're really done with." I burst into tears, knowing she'd gone right to the heart of the matter, and I was not going to get off easily by simply leaving my marriage. Whatever I was bumping up against would follow me to the next relationship, and the next, and the next, ad infinitum, unless I faced it.

I wish I could say that I figured out the answer to what I was "done with" right then, during that session, or even in the next few, but I didn't. It took hard and ongoing work, but over time, I realized that I was through with living a half-life, trapped in fear and entrenched patterns of self-abandonment and self-abnegation. I came to see that relating with Rick may trigger a reaction in me, but *he* does not cause it. It arises from within me, based on a host of prior experiences and faulty assumptions. Indeed, I find that engaging in intimate relationship is like dwelling in a hall of mirrors.

Everywhere I turn, I see my reflection, and finally accepting that fact has brought a certain peace to my body and soul. I no longer exhaust myself with the impossibly ludicrous task of what essentially amounts to my gazing in the looking glass and trying to make the image I see there into Rick's. It's empowering, really, to lay down that struggle and pick up curiosity instead. When something difficult surfaces in me—an unpleasant thought, emotion, or sensation—about Rick or our relationship, I now peer closely at it and ask myself, *What part of my shadow—the aspects of myself hidden from my consciousness, as Jung would assert—is this evoking? What difficult facet of myself do I need to acknowledge, explore, tend to, or transform?*

To manage this colossal conversion of perspective—of releasing Rick from my laser focus and turning it instead onto myself so that I could take full responsibility for my experience of reality and for my life—I had to pull away from my husband somewhat. It wasn't something I intentionally set out to do, but I gradually distanced myself from him physically, mentally, and emotionally to get the space I needed to tackle my demons. Though I couldn't have named the dynamic at the time of its onset, the deepest, wisest part of myself must have sensed that I needed to separate to individuate.

This key step in the human maturation process is meant to occur much earlier in life than at age sixty (during adolescence and the early twenties perhaps?) so that one enters union with another person from a place of wholeness. Ideally, two fully formed adults come together, creating a third reality, which is their relationship. But, as I had painfully learned, my early life strayed far from any ideal, and it felt to me like a case of better late than never. Just as I knew that my continued health and well-being required it, I understood that any chance of creating a healthier more fulfilling paradigm with Rick also hung on continuing my own personal healing work.

At the same time, I understood in a deeper way than ever before that a relationship is a two-way street and that responsibility for creating our less-than-optimal partnership didn't fall solely on me. The more I learned about trauma, the easier it was to understand that Rick carried into our union his own burdensome baggage from childhood, and that he bore an equal share of accountability for where we found ourselves. When I spoke that truth to him, he was able to hear it, and over time, as I gained surer footing and Rick himself engaged in self-inquiry, we began to discuss the evolving energy between us more openly, taking baby steps in the direction of truer intimacy. Any new territory worth exploring is often fraught with danger, and our earliest conversations about our marriage were often only partially helpful, and sometimes downright hurtful. But as the months progressed, we honed our skills of relating to ourselves and to each other, and—for better or for worse—we arrived at the uncommon place of simultaneously acknowledging our deep love and our uncertain future.

Of course, COVID threw its own wrench in the works of our process. It hit at the precise time we'd decided to get some outside help through Imago Relationship Therapy—designed to help couples bring greater consciousness to their relationship by understanding each other's feelings, childhood traumas, and wounding more empathetically—shutting down that avenue almost before it began. We both felt thwarted and resentful at first. In retrospect, we've discovered that particular work probably wasn't right for us anyway, with its emphasis on developing communication and mutual respect, which we were already far ahead on. The troublesome virus actually saved us a lot of time and money when it forced us, by shelter-in-place mandated proximity, to face ourselves and each other and find our own way.

We sat down and discussed what we'd need to do, in lieu of therapy, to help our relationship along. We both committed to work on our own personal healing—in whatever way felt appropriate to each of us—and to meeting together weekly, if possible, for focused dialogue. Our express intent for these sessions was threefold: to share our individual processes, raise issues in the relationship, and explore mutually beneficial solutions. We've stuck to the pattern quite faithfully, allowing for flexibility as circumstances arise that alter the time and energy we each have available.

I've found this path of working on our coupleship that we created for ourselves alternately painful, freeing, blessed, liberating, agonizing, difficult, confusing, joyous, and more. I wouldn't trade a moment of it for any amount of riches because it has led me to a few simple truths. One of which is that the future of our marriage boils down to the issue of what each of us wants for our *own* future. Of course, because I love him, I want all kinds of things for Rick. Like for him to explore and heal his traumatic past. To do the deep work for himself that his support has enabled me to undertake, knowing as I do that it leads to greater wholeness and joy. (I especially wish it for him now, as studies are starting to confirm that clearing and treating unresolved trauma may be preventive medicine equally as important for long-term health as good sleep, nutritious eating, and regular exercise.)

What I have come to understand is that, ultimately, what *I* desire for him bears no relevance whatsoever to his life. My acceptance of that fact is one of the ways I am choosing to love him. What matters in our partnership is what he wants for himself, and of course, what I want for myself, and whether those two visions can coexist. As Amit Ray has said, "The true miracle lies in our eagerness to allow, appreciate, and honor the uniqueness and freedom of each sentient being to sing the song of their heart." Rick's melody is different from mine, and I respect that reality, just as he honors the distinctiveness of my own. But can our music blend harmoniously? Neither of us wants to live amidst tonal discordance, nor do we desire that for the other. We truly wish what's best for each of us, even if that means we might need to let one another go. Isn't that really the essence of love? According to Maya Angelou, "Love liberates. It doesn't just hold—that's ego— love liberates!"

To figure out what one deeply and truly wants, however, isn't easy, but I felt we had to try. So, one day, curious about what Rick was thinking and feeling, I inquired, "About our marriage, what do you want for your future?"

After a moment's pause to collect himself (at the time, I still tended to jump rather abruptly into the deep end of the pool), he said, "I'm not sure. I feel like a lot of what we have is good. But there's also a lot missing."

"I agree," I readily replied.

"I don't want to go through the pain of a breakup, or try to explain it to my old and frail parents, or start all over again with another person, or deal with any of this in the midst of the pandemic. It all feels like too much. I don't know. It's like we're two dear old friends helping each other through COVID. Maybe that's enough for right now."

"I love that image of us," I told him, and left our encounter, which only lasted a few minutes longer, with a warm feeling in my heart. A couple of days later, though, I realized I was also feeling unsettled by our conversation, so I sat down with my journal to see if I could get at the unnamed feelings bubbling up inside me. Not long into writing, I uncovered anger. I was peeved at Rick because he hadn't answered my question. He hadn't described what he wanted, he'd told me only what he *didn't* want or what he was willing to settle for.

As you may have already guessed, my annoyance with him didn't last but the briefest of moments as I quickly grasped that his response upset me because it held up such a shining mirror to my own inability to name what *I* wanted. I had to admit I didn't have an answer to my question either, once again encountering that hard to swallow but ultimately delicious gift of intimate relationship: in it, we come face-to-face with ourselves, like it or not. In that moment of realization, I committed with vigor to discovering the answer to my own question for myself. I reaffirmed my knowledge that only then would I have any hope of creating a fulfilling life, marriage or no.

At the start of this undertaking, I envisioned compiling a list of components or sketching out an image of my "ideal life." Almost immediately, however, the inquiry morphed within me from *What do I want?* into *What is life asking of me?* This change in questions reflects the most profound shift in orientation that has occurred within me over these healing years. In working so hard to find my Self, I also lost it. In a most exhilarating way. By opening to the fullness of the direct human experience—with all its agony and ecstasy—I tumbled into the realm of the beyond. By feeling into the energy of *my* life, I encountered the energy that runs through *all* life, and I now sense myself as an instrument of that force. I am responsible for keeping my instrument tuned and ready—through my various personal practices of awareness, embodiment, self-care, and spiritual growth—so that the music of the spheres can play through me with beauty and power, but I am not in control of the symphony.

Let me wax less esoteric and offer a concrete example of what I just described. As I see it, I didn't choose writing, I was led to it. When I began my healing journey, I set my heart and mind on the desire to live deeply and purposefully in the world and then followed the path gradually laid out before me, completely uncertain of the destination. Relying on the guidance of inner wisdom, which I've come to understand as my experience of a greater universal intelligence, I took each outward step revealed along the way and arrived at the unexpected. If anyone had said to me a few years ago that in my early sixties I'd write and then consider publishing a book, I'd have told them the notion was ludicrous. But here I am, working toward exactly that, because it's what Life—with a capital *L*—has asked of me.

To return to Rick's and my story, I realized that this fundamental approach to existence I'd cultivated was not one he shared and might render the gap between us unbridgeable. Despite that fact, I knew I had to show up in my marriage in ways that were true to me, to my new understanding of who I am and how I need to live. Because I possessed the same desire to live as deeply and purposefully in the arena of intimate relationship as in the realms of creativity and livelihood, I had to trust that, as I explored more fully and released more completely into that intention, the way would be made clear.

I decided to rededicate myself—yet again—to my personal healing work, knowing that, over time, I would come to gain clarity about what Life was asking of me regarding us as well. It remained to be seen whether that would be to stay married; to consciously uncouple—to borrow Katherine Woodward Thomas's brilliant concept—making room for the possibility of a new relationship; or to move in some yet unimagined direction. And, of course, I acknowledged that Rick trod his own parallel path of deciding for himself what was right for him, with equal impact for our coupleship.

A huge turning point for us came when I went away by myself in December 2020 on my writer's retreat in Lone Pine. That brief interlude bore fruit not just for this book, but also, quite unexpectedly, for our marriage, in a way beyond my wildest imaginings. It started with my letting go of the last remnants of a fairy tale I didn't even realize I was hanging on to. One evening, about a week into my trip, after I'd finished with writing for the day, cooked and eaten my dinner, and cleaned up after myself, I decided to poke around the internet resources I'd bookmarked on women's empowerment. After some time down the rabbit hole, just as I was becoming weary and considered going to bed, I encountered a reference to a book I'd never read by Barbara Stanny entitled *Prince Charming Isn't Coming*, and was jolted awake by the phrase. It jumped out at me and lit up my brain.

I realized in an instant that, despite being a sixty-two-year-old, intelligent woman, and a committed feminist, a little girl lurked inside me who still believed the fairy tale: Prince Charming was out there, and I just needed to find him. I saw how this unconscious—until that very moment—desire had operated in subtle ways throughout my life. Even recently, for example, in how I had zeroed in on Rick as the "problem" when I first started to heal, instead of looking within myself for what I needed. If I didn't somehow believe in Prince Charming, Rick's "faults" would have seemed irrelevant. Of course, I've managed to transcend much of the fairy tale's falsehood, but that evening, while on retreat, I recognized its final remaining vestige and decided I needed to jettison it, for good.

And I was ready to chuck it overboard, let me tell you, because it was causing me unnecessary pain; Rick too. Only two weeks before I had left for Lone Pine, we marked our twenty-eighth wedding anniversary with a companionable walk on the beach, followed by a tender conversation. We sat huddled together on two stools pulled up to the kitchen peninsula. I reached for the card perched there addressed to me in Rick's strong hand, distinctively all caps, and holding it close to my chest, slumped against the upholstered back of the stool.

"True confessions time," I said sadly. "I didn't get you a card. I spent an hour at the store, reading practically every single one, and I couldn't find anything I felt okay about buying. They said things like 'Together forever,' and we may not be. Or they were ridiculously mushy. Or insulting. I just couldn't do it and feel authentic."

"Don't worry. It doesn't matter to me. Besides, wait until you read the one I found," he replied with a smile, nodding at the card I held in my hand. Thus prompted, I removed the card from the envelope. On the front it said, "You know me better than anyone, and you still love me." Inside it said, "So I have to ask, what's wrong with you?"

"How perfect." I laughed. "If I'd seen one like that, I'd have bought it!" After a pause, I added, "At one point, I thought about getting a thank-you card, because that seemed so much more appropriate. But I didn't. I guess I just want to say that to you."

"Okay," he said, and waited.

I took a deep breath and began, "Thank you for loving me so faithfully all these years, and for sticking with me through this roller coaster ride of healing. No matter what happens between us—whether we stay together or get divorced—I will always love you and be grateful to you," I finished, with tears streaming down my face and a hard lump choking my throat.

"Me too," he said, clearly moved himself.

Despite the strong affinity between us, somehow, we'd gotten ourselves stuck at a place of pain. During this conversation, and previous ones, both of us had expressed gut-wrenching sadness at what felt like the death of passion beyond resuscitation, and we'd named several times the aching possibility that to enable both of us to get all that we desired in an intimate relationship, we might need to split and seek out other partners. Here is where I discovered that insidious fairy tale's lie operating stealthily beneath the surface, in me and in Rick. It dawned on me that the myth of Prince Charming prevents a woman from full maturity, with its implication that a person outside herself holds the key to her happiness. And the presumably more sophisticated myth of a soul mate—something Rick stated he wanted me to have and, I believe, wouldn't have minded for himself—just delivers a nuance of that same invalid externalizing message to all.

Both iterations are manifestly untrue, and I was ready to lay them down. I finally understood what Gloria had been trying to help me see all this time: the key to my happiness lies within *me*, completely. I am my own beloved; my pleasure—in life and in love—is my responsibility; and I need look to no one else but myself for the source of a satisfying and fulfilling relationship. Assuming common values and barring nothing untoward, the other person essentially doesn't matter. Here I was, fortunate enough to live with a flesh-and-blood man for whom I felt abundant love in my heart, and who felt the same for me. Good God, how many people were that lucky? And I had come perilously close to throwing away that precious gift. I just needed to get on with it—to drop the fairy story and grow up, take total responsibility for my own happiness, and do whatever I could to find a way back to us, wholly. That night I vowed that when I returned home, I would tell Rick that I was all in. If he would have me, I was ready to commit wholeheartedly to creating a marriage that would feed and fuel us both.

I'm happy to report I fulfilled that vow, and Rick received me and my renewed commitment to him with open arms. We agreed to release one another from fairy tales and myths—and the lie of perfection that hides at their centers—and begin a new phase in our long journey together. We're working hard on what we call our "grand experiment" in relationship regeneration: learning daily how to love ourselves completely so that we come to one another full and pouring forth, not empty and clamoring; how to be authentically ourselves, while being completely with the other; how to be truly interdependent and coregulating. So far, so good. But I have a sense the hard work has only just begun and, given some painful factors in our shared journey that I'll get into in the next chapter, I'm not even tempted to say, "And they lived happily ever after." I'm laying down *all* parts of the fairy tale and instead picking up the practice of living comfortably with the unknown.

CHAPTER 12

Sex in the Sixties (And I Don't Mean the 1960s)

Not all couples who lose sexual intimacy and want to get it back must contend with the shadow of rape and sexual violence, but Rick and I did, which, of course, complicated our story greatly. Since I shared early on in this book that I am a multiple-incident survivor, you may have surmised that those traumas gave rise to struggles with my sexuality. And you would be right, to some degree. While each specific incident, with its own unique flavor of overwhelm, chipped away at my ability to be fully present to the life-giving energy of physical union, in truth, a much earlier and subtler transgression against my person prepared the ground for those more outwardly violent incidents and required the deepest healing.

As I began my curative work, *I was robbed, and I mean to have my due!* became a kind of rallying cry of mine. I never actually uttered it aloud, but its powerful message quietly underlay my exploration and restoration efforts. As I came to understand it, two actors in a long-ago specific incident stole from me my most precious treasure—my innate healthy sexuality—at a very young age, and despite what society might say about a woman of my years, I intended to get it back, with interest. Remember my MSC backdraft experience of an overpowering, visceral sense of shame triggered by a childhood memory? It was in that moment I encountered the root of my prolonged struggle, and my quest for sexual reparations began.

As is the nature of traumatic memory, some of the details appear fuzzy, some cut crystal clear. If I zoom in, I see myself at maybe five years old. I'm standing naked in my tiny little bedroom, filled with the sense of enchanted loftiness being there always brings me—my window towering as it does three stories above the back-yard, looking out into the lacy green treetops. It's near the middle of the day and probably summer because a strong sun streams in that same window, deliciously warming my bare skin. Sounds of kids playing outside—muffled voices punctuated by shrieks of glee, a swing creaking, a ball thudding on dirt—tickle my ears.

Widening the lens on this memory, another person is in the room with me. A boy, Jeff, slightly younger than I. He's also naked, but when he speaks, the aura of innocent, sensuous delight begins to dissipate. A chilly unease rises in me as he asks me to do things I don't want to do. When I balk, he hurls childish insults and taunts my hesitancy. When I persist in my unwillingness, he amps up—no longer asking, now demanding. He bullies with shoves and threatens in a shrill tone, and though we are the same size, I feel scared and comply with his demands: I drop to my knees, spread the cheeks of his buttocks, and kiss his anus; I take his scrotum into my mouth, feeling acutely discomfited. Just wanting it all to end.

Suddenly, the door to my room bursts open, and my mother appears. My heart lifts, but only for an instant, as the full force of her shock and disgust bears down on me before I can choke out a sound. "What is wrong with you? How could you? Get your clothes on this instant and get back outside," she hisses at me through clenched teeth, eyes wide and cheeks blazing. Then she turns away and rushes off. That's where the memory abruptly ends. I've tried, but I cannot access any other visual or auditory details, any further traces of interpersonal exchange, any inkling of more thoughts that arose. But, while my mind may have gone blank, my body clearly remembered what I felt like in the aftermath: over fifty years after this incident—when learning how to love myself triggered the horrifying flashback—I found myself consumed by shame, feeling utterly condemned and alone, dirty, worthless, wanting to disappear from the world.

Strangely enough, or not so strangely maybe, what bubbles up in me as I write about this scene is compassion. A great deal of compassion for all three players. For myself, of course, but also for that tormented boy and for my poor mama. This was no benevolent example of childhood sex play, of innate curiosity about the differences between girls and boys, of innocent exploration of bodies. I shudder to think what Jeff must have already endured in his short life—probably at the hands of a known and trusted adult—for him to behave as he did. He channeled an injurious energy far older than his tender years, traveling down—for generations, perhaps—through his perpetrator's family, which may have been his own. Wherever he is now, if he's still alive, I hope he's found release from his traumas and a healing of his body, mind, and spirit.

Unfortunately, my mother never found either release or healing while on this planet, dying almost twenty years ago at age seventy-nine from the slow suicide of addiction to alcohol and cigarettes. I have no proof—save a gut instinct I've learned the hard way to trust—but I suspect she endured some form of sexual trauma, maybe even more than once in her lifetime, like I did. In any case, obviously triggered into a mass of shame, disgust, anger, fear, and whatever else by what she thought she saw when she opened my bedroom door, she was incapable of stepping outside herself and coming to the aid of her young daughter. I know—all too well—what it feels like to reckon with failing one's child, and my heart goes out to her. That said, though, she's the one who put the nail in my coffin that day. And I have rightfully claimed and worked through my anger and grief at her abandonment, so that I could forgive her posthumously and find peace for myself.

You see, while what transpired between Jeff and me was hurtful and ugly, a skillful response from a safe adult would have kept it outside the realm of trauma. In fact, in this instance, my mother's very reaction constituted the life-changing overwhelm of my nervous system, not what transpired between Jeff and me. All I need to do is reconsider Gabor Maté's idea of trauma as separation from self to grasp the truth of that assertion. My mother's swift condemnation ensured I would remain split off from my own clear instincts and feelings and, instead, become hopelessly entangled in hers. Recall Saint-Laurent and Bird's definition of trauma, "too much, too soon, or too fast for our nervous system to handle, *especially if we can't reach a successful resolution.*" (Emphasis mine.) My mother's inability to discuss what happened meant that nothing in my experience was cleared up, answered, or understood. Or look to Peter Levine's own description from *In an Unspoken Voice* of how careful attention to the needs of his body—in the presence of a caring witness—helped keep an accident from becoming lodged as trauma when he was hit by a car. The scorching finality of my mother's turning away from my body is what burned trauma into my cells and circuitry.

What happens in the immediate aftermath of a stressor makes all the difference, and what my little girl needed most back then was help with integration. Imagine this: The door opens. My mother takes in the scene. Noticing the strong emotions arising within her body, she pauses to take a deep, calming breath, then enters the room to inquire and guide. With that shift alone, my whole life likely would have been different. My healthy sexuality saved in a matter of seconds—in the time it took her to inhale. But my beleaguered mother was incapable of centered presence. Not wanting to waste any of my energy on fruitless wishing it were otherwise, as a purposeful part of my healing, I've stepped into her place. I've played out in my mind several iterations of my adult-self coming to the aid of my scared, confused, hurting little girl. Each rework unfolds slightly differently, but they all share common threads: I provide physical comfort for her distressed body, affirm all her complicated feelings, and talk with her about her right to personal boundaries in a way that's comprehensible to a young child. (And, of course, in this imaginal reclamation process, I also handle Jeff compassionately.)

Going into the past in this way constituted an important piece of healing work. I've done similar processing of the two rapes I endured as well as various incidents of sexual assault that peppered my adolescence and young adulthood. After all, as the saying goes, "We can't heal what we don't feel." I had to go back in time to embrace the pain of what happened, release stuck energy, entertain better outcomes. But all that effort represents only a beginning to the healing. The permanent rewiring of my neural pathways to liberate my body and empower my sexuality also required new experiences in the present, and for that I took the work into my own hands—literally. Miraculously, I never received negative messages about masturbation, which was perhaps the one advantage to growing up in a family where sex was never discussed—ever. So, I didn't hesitate in this work, nor did I have to wrestle with any moral dilemma around it. My only discomfort surrounded my husband and the sacrifice he made in giving me the space I needed to heal. In the end, I knew he was choosing to stay with me, and that he, too, had hands.

Before continuing, I'd like to state clearly that, despite the wounding early on, sex was not all bad for me over the years. Again, shades of gray. As can be common with victims of sexual trauma, my early warped imprinting led me into risky behaviors such as promiscuity, into the misidentification of seduction as power, and into a kind of twisted push-pull approach to the whole undertaking that continually buffeted and sometimes endangered me. Even so, especially as I matured beyond adolescence and young adulthood, I managed to make some positive connections, have some healthy fun, and experience a transcendent moment or two along the way, like when Rick and I conceived our son. With the insights from my awakening and a close examination of my past, however, I became aware that even under my more wholesome encounters lurked an element of struggle not innate to the dynamic—a taint of shame, even disgust, underlying it all. I committed to purging that stain from my body and soul and sensed I could only accomplish the initial stage of that cure alone (with therapeutic support, of course).

Sexual desire had begun to wane years earlier in my relationship with Rick, but when I began the work of tackling these specific wounds of my past, it completely disappeared—dried up entirely—in the face of my towering grief. Assuming it long gone, I mourned the ecstatic potential of the nubile body of my youth and pretty much resigned myself to a sexless future. I remember saying to my then therapist Livia, "I think I'm done with all that."

"Sure," she replied. After a moment's pause, she added, "It's a matter of deciding what's right for you. I've worked with plenty of women who've lived happily in their later years without sex," affirming my declaration of possible celibacy as perfectly legitimate.

"Okay," I said, feeling validated.

"I've also worked with many older women who live happily *with* sex," she continued, raising another possibility. "And the secret to that choice is lots and lots of lube," she finished up with a knowing smile and a twinkle in her eye.

I couldn't help but grin back at her remark.

With this brief exchange, Livia artfully managed to help me accept exactly how I was feeling in that moment and to simultaneously leave the door of my mind open, showing how she really was the perfect person to start this work with. You may recall that, originally, her Body Scan Meditation recording drew me to her while I was taking MBSR. In part, it was her obvious comfort with the human body and sexuality that had appealed to me. While other presenters used euphemisms like "organs of reproduction and elimination" when guiding our awareness around our pelvic area, Livia dove right in, inviting us to pay attention to sensations in our genitals and anus. I found that very refreshing, comforting somehow, even though I didn't fully understand why at the time. Later, as we engaged in our brief therapeutic work together, I experienced her easy frankness as both life affirming of my body and curative to my soul. She set me up well to go further with my sexual healing in somatic therapy.

As I did that deeper work, my previous harsh rallying cry, which was focused outward on what others had done to me and on seeking justice, turned into something gentler and more inwardly focused. Gradually, a new phrase emerged in the form of a question I would ask myself, over and over, becoming a mantra incanted throughout my days: *What does my body love?* Those five words distilled my quest to its very essence: Through trauma therapy, 5R, and other somatic practices, I sought to discover what stirs my juices, gets me going, brings me fully alive—what feels good to me as an exquisitely embodied animal—and to live from that place.

Not surprisingly then, as my trauma healing progressed, sexual desire resurfaced. It may sound funny, but I almost didn't recognize it at first. Partly because I hadn't been specifically looking for it and partly because it had been dormant such a long while, but mostly because it felt different this time around. There was a purity to it, arising spontaneously from within me at unexpected moments. And a totality to it, encompassing my whole self— body, mind, and spirit. Qualities which had not characterized it so strongly before.

Initially, physical yearning bubbled up during an experience of partner dancing in a 5R class. While momentarily disconcerting— after all, I was a married woman, and this was *not* my husband—I quickly understood that the man himself was irrelevant. So, I relaxed into the feelings, into my heartbeat rising, my breath coming quicker and shallower, my chest opening, my back arching, my groin warming and pulsing with energy. The self-awareness and maturity gained thus far through my healing journey easily kept me from misinterpreting this encounter as anything more than it was. I come alive in the dance—fully, all parts of me—and I connect to the divine, so of course my sensuality would naturally stir. The exquisitely delicious sensation was so welcome to me, like a flowing spring in an arid desert, and I offered a silent prayer of gratitude for it, "Ah, here it is. Here is my life force. Praise be," and for my partner, for what he was—a mirror into my own being. Then I went home and celebrated by myself.

Like on that day, as desire continued to reawaken, I celebrated it in large and small ways: bodily, through deep explorations in self-pleasuring; mentally, through reading breakthrough books on female sexuality; and spiritually, through exploring resources on Tantra and other holy frameworks. Slowly, I came to understand my sexuality as something sacred, core to my very self, and foundational to my total well-being. I was able to decide that, even though my breasts may reflect five decades of gravity's relentless pull and my pubic hair may be gray and wispy, I was definitely *not* "done with all that," as I had declared earlier to Livia.

The dynamic of feeling sexual arousal outside my marriage happened again only once more but presented a greater challenge the second time. After that first encounter, I had purposefully thrown myself into the delightful work of cultivating a vibrant sexuality, so I guess it's no surprise that what arose in me now wasn't just a bubbling brook of desire but a raging torrent. And this time, as a further complicating dimension, my feelings were echoed by the other.

When I first met Angel, we were stark naked, both having wound up, along with several others, in the same clothing-optional hot springs pool shortly after arriving at Esalen for five-day stays in the summer of 2019—me to attend a 5R workshop, he on his own self-guided retreat. I delight in Esalen's welcoming attitude toward nudity in designated areas, which allows me to tap into my deep reverence for the varied beauty of the human body. His, so like Michelangelo's *David* though rendered in warm mahogany flesh instead of cold white marble, definitely moved me. But what I remember most about that delicious hour-long soak, was listening raptly to all the bathers' stories and engaging in lively exchanges with various folks, about what had drawn each of us to this special place at this particular time in our lives.

It wasn't until a few hours later, when I found myself, now fully clothed, sitting at the same table at dinner, continuing the getting-to-know-you process begun in the pool, that the attraction I felt toward Angel began to dawn on me. Another kind of nakedness seemed to permeate our exchange—a baring of soul and a revealing of mind. Walking back to my room later that evening, I was fairly vibrating, head-to-toe, with a powerful energy, aware that something important was brewing inside of me. The next day, without design and despite being in different programs on campus, our paths crossed continually—early morning, in the pools, at mealtimes, our very biorhythms seemingly in sync—and every time, we'd quickly resume our open sharing and frank conversation, an intimacy growing between us with startling ease. Each interaction amped up my energy, and I sensed he might be having a similar experience.

On the second full day, finding ourselves yet again across from one another in one of the hot spring pools, this time alone, Angel looked me directly in the eye and said tentatively, "I'm attracted to you. I've imagined being physical with you." After a brief pause, he added, "And I sense that you might feel the same way."

"Yes," I replied quietly, returning his gaze. "I feel similarly."

"Okay," he sighed, relief at bringing it into the open relaxing his face into a smile.

I could feel my whole body let go as well, the tension I'd been holding subsiding, and I returned his smile. It felt good to name with words what had become palpable in the very air around us. However, despite having known each other for less than forty-eight hours, our instant rapport had led us to discover that we were in similar painful places in our romantic lives: both in love with our partners back home, yet struggling in our respective relationships with issues of sexual connection. And now, here between us, pulsed an acknowledged passion. A more perfect recipe for betrayal could not have been devised.

Except we opted to do something completely different with the ingredients. In utter faithfulness to our respective absent beloveds, we consciously chose to examine our attraction—from a safe distance—with curiosity, integrity, maturity, compassion, and intentional presence, to explore it for what it might mean for each of us in our individual lives. (Ah, the benefits of being older and wiser.) We did not allow ourselves to get swept away by mindlessly acting on it, nor did we shy away from it by trying to deny its existence. Instead, we just lived with it there between us, matter-of-factly, often finding humor in it. I came to see that Angel simply served as another mirror into my own sexuality, eminently more powerful than that first one, and in it I glimpsed the image of my highest and most alive self. In fact, it was thanks to the energy between Angel and me that I experienced my first full-body orgasm, my first taste of ecstasy.

One evening, upon returning to my room, I realized my entire body was buzzing with vibrant aliveness, simply from having been in Angel's presence. Since I had the space all to myself now—my roommate having left the 5R program two days early, perhaps not coincidentally—I decided to do something with my exhilaration. To celebrate it. So, I spent over an hour caressing every inch of my body, delighting in the sensual touches, building intensity, and then backing off teasingly, over and over, driving myself mad with desire, as I imagined he might have done if we'd made a different choice, until I seemed to lose consciousness of anything but sensation—my breasts aching, my nipples erect and straining, my vulva engorged and yawning open, wetness oozing down my thighs, energy vibrating every cell that constituted me. When I finally burst forth into blazing light, a powerful electricity arcing through my entire being, I cried out in amazement. So, this is what was possible.

I have thanked God, the Universe, Spirit, whomever, so many times for sending me "my" Angel, whose last name I don't know, whom I'll never see again, and whom I touched but twice in brief, chaste hugs of appreciation—once after a particularly meaningful conversation about shame and once upon saying good-bye—who, simply with his bright reflection, returned me to the fullness of my sexuality. I left Esalen with the sense that, over time, I would come to know if Life was asking me to share it with the man who was currently my husband. If so, hallelujah! If not, well, then I would know that my path forward lay in a different direction, because there was no going back now. I wanted this in my life in the biggest way.

I also knew that I still had healing to do before I would be physically ready to engage fully with a man. So, sex in the sixties remained a solo affair for a while, but a glorious one. By choosing to continue to abstain from relations with my husband, while simultaneously cultivating my sexuality as much as possible on my own, I gave myself the gift of absolute safety—a sense I'd never possessed before in this realm because of my past, not even with committed partners, including Rick. It liberated me, enabling the discovery of dimensions of sexuality I'd not previously experienced, which I sensed might only be deepened in actual union with a partner when the time felt right. It also showed me how intimately pleasure and pain are connected: I knew I'd found the heights of the former because I'd dared to descend into the depths of the latter.

The truth of that knowing echoed loudly in my body several months ago. During therapy, while tending to yet more stuck trauma energy—this time in my other shoulder—my second rapist's face suddenly emerged unbidden in my mind's eye, in full technicolor detail. Despite my having known him well, in previous flashbacks, his visage had appeared indistinct. All I'd had to work with was the sense of his bodily form. Now, with his image finally whole, the energy that flowed through me was nearly overwhelming, tumbling about in a whirl of fierce emotions, alternately fiery and icy. A few days later, when I took myself in my own hands, the rapturous sounds I uttered as climax neared turned into howls of grief and pain, my orgasm ushering me into racking sobs as my potent life force washed away that old agonizing hurt.

Shortly thereafter, in therapy, while discussing the mix of emotions that arose in that powerful, cleansing experience, it became clear that I was still tangled up in my wounded mother's feelings about sex. Gloria prescribed the medicine of ritual. As you know, I'd already gone there in my imagination—with reworkings of the original childhood scene of wounding—but now it was time to bring this unshackling of my little girl into the somatic realm where the deepest healing takes place. Indigenous people across the globe have understood the transformative power of rite and ceremony for millennia, and I decided to harness that energy for my own well-being. When the day came where I knew I'd have the house to myself for hours, I began.

I assembled colored pencils, patterned paper, cardstock, pinking shears, any creative supplies I could think of, and set to work crafting individual pieces of word art for SHAME, DISGUST, FEAR, and ANGER. When I was done, I attached a long piece of yarn to each emotion card and jumbled them all up in a big, tangled mass. I placed a photo of myself at age three—one that I call my tiger baby picture because in it I'm on fire with animal life, sporting a gleeful grin and a mischievous gleam in my eye—on the floor in the center of my room and then covered it over with that snarled mess of my mother's feelings. I lit a candle, put on some soulful music, and the stage was set. Without a plan but guided by Spirit, I danced much of the ritual, slowly untangling the yarn, separating each emotion card, carefully setting it aside once it was loosed, tenderly revealing my pure and joyous self underneath, unfettered—finally clear of all the ugliness my mother had inadvertently but tragically laid on me so long ago, finally released from my false prison. I consecrated my freedom with orgasm. Then I bore the emotion cards outside, burned them, and placed their ashes under my favorite tree to nurture it, ending with a bow to that powerful metaphor of growth.

Engaging in this ritual constituted an enormous breakthrough for me. Immediately in its wake, I felt lighter, cleaner, happier, like something that I hadn't even realized was tightly squeezing the life out of me had finally let go. I could breathe and be, with a new ease, and that sense of unbinding from my mother only grew as the days, weeks, and months went by. It seemed to permeate my whole life—my dancing, my writing, my relationships—and I felt the expansiveness most in how I now began to look at and interact with Rick. It was with this background awareness of something powerfully shifting within me that I went off on my writer's retreat to Lone Pine and fell into the arms of that liberating insight about not needing Prince Charming.

It got even juicier as I continued to spend those December days entirely on my own, tuning into myself and my rhythms, doing exactly what I wanted, when I wanted, and how I wanted. Because, what I began to want—to hunger for in a way I hadn't for so long—was to see and be with my husband. The bodily rush of that yearning was a pleasure almost too exquisite to receive. I immediately flashed on the saying "Absence makes the heart grow fonder," and laughed, wondering if there might be some enduring truth at the base of that trite adage.

I received the answer to my musing after supper one evening. Stretched out on the couch, reading *The Wild Woman's Way* by Michaela Boehm, a psychotherapist and Tantric lineage holder, I gaped in amazement at how the Universe does so love to send me confirmation when I'm on the right track. In her chapter entitled "Relationships," I found a new way to understand Rick's and my story, a way out of pathologizing it and into celebrating it, a way forward. According to Boehm, the state we were in—where the love, respect, resonance, and communication are incredibly strong, but the erotic spark is gone—was not the sign of our relationship failing.

The lost attraction was more likely due to the rich commonality and familiarity we shared—essential elements of a loving relationship, but diametrically opposed to the friction needed to fire passion. I felt cheered by Boehm's assertion that for Rick and me, reigniting the flame was entirely possible simply by adopting different behaviors, applying new skills, and spending our time together less mindlessly. This idea reminded me of a TED Talk by Esther Perel that I'd encountered only weeks before my trip. Perel, a psychotherapist and author of *Mating in Captivity*, similarly contends that success in monogamous relationships depends on honoring the creative tension between the human needs for both safety and freedom, an idea that resonated with me as I listened to her speak.

When I read that Boehm often recommends to couples struggling similarly to us, that individuals have their own rooms, if space allows, and find ways to separate activities and lives to some degree, I knew I'd found a place for Rick and me to start, if he was willing. To be sure, this idea had been creeping up on me for some time. Recently via Perel, but really, it had started well over a year before, when I discovered that my newish but quickly dear friend Val and her husband happily reside in different houses most of each week. Then, while reading Judith Orloff's *The Empath's Survival Guide*, I encountered a frank discussion of the author's need to have a room separate from her partner's to maintain her well-being and her ability to relate intimately.

Instead of thinking to myself, *Well, that's weird. Couples should share a room,* which is what I would have thought previously, I casually thought *Hm, that's interesting.* I was beginning to see there were many ways to "do" intimate relationship and to understand that what really matters are the unique needs of each couple, not some prescribed social convention. Finally, shortly before leaving for Lone Pine, the phrase "trial separation" had popped into my head when I thought about my solo retreat—not necessarily as preparation for divorce, which it denotes in legalese, but as an important exercise in living apart after nine months of pandemic-induced 24/7 togetherness. Separate was clearly a theme here. Well, good God, of course it was. To heal from trauma, I had had to energetically separate from my husband to do the deep work of individuation, and it had ultimately led me back to him. So why would that same movement not hold the key to our sexuality as well?

When I returned home from retreat, and we renewed our commitment to each other, we both agreed that the trickiest part of what lay ahead was overcoming the physical chasm between us. We'd hung out for years now as dear friends—without benefits—and neither of us could imagine how to bridge that painful, yawning gap. It felt utterly daunting, but with neither of us willing to continue to live as an asexual couple, we needed to at least see if it was possible. So—hoping the resources I'd come across were onto something—we began to lead more separate lives, starting with occupying different bedrooms and bathrooms, to see if it would help our togetherness.

These lifestyle changes had been in place for less than a month when I got a vision one morning. Vivid images of Rick and me flooded my mind: we were naked in a bed, caressing each other—no more, just caressing—and I realized how starved I was for even just that exquisite pleasure, for the simple act of touching and being touched in love. I felt like I'd found a place to start. I approached Rick after lunch, the first time we'd seen each other that day. "I'd like to invite you on a date tonight," I said.

"Oh?" he replied, momentarily startled. "Okay," he went on, regaining his calm. "What did you have in mind? I mean, with the COVID spike and everything shut down again, it's not like we can go anywhere."

"No, I know. I was thinking of something closer to home. I'm going back to writing now, probably until around four, then I'm going to go for a walk and have dinner and relax on my own. How about you come to my room at seven, for a play-date, for an hour?"

"Sure," he said, ever eager, though I could see some uncertainty in his gaze.

"Would you like to know what I have in mind, or would you like to be surprised?" I asked. Visibly relieved, he opted for the former, and after I shared my vision with him, said he'd be delighted to join me for an hour's experiment in just touching.

I can't speak for him, but for me, the six-plus-hour run-up to our appointed time proved delicious, anticipation mounting, just like it had when we'd first come together so long ago. I savored my pre-date alone time, purposefully tuning into my thoughts, sensations, and emotions, and delighting in the ritual of preparation—showering, anointing my skin with rose-scented lotion, donning a silky robe, lighting a candle, putting on soft music. By the time Rick knocked on my door, my body was so ready to give and to receive the pleasure of human contact, with no thought to outcome, that I felt not the slightest embarrassment nor uncertainty, only excitement. After slowly shedding our clothes and climbing under the sheet together, our bodies took over, and we spent a blissful hour lost in one another, naturally flowing right past our original intent to just touch into a deep physical reconnection, as if we had never, ever grown apart.

To think that we had almost thrown this possibility away. That we had been so stuck in our minds, trying to "figure out" how to get back to each other, when all we really needed to do was get out of our heads and into our bodies for the answer. They knew what to do. As our time together that evening drew to a close, my husband, the cyclist, said, "I guess it's like riding a bike. You never forget." And, in saying amen to that sentiment the next morning while journaling, I almost wrote that I was grateful for our happy ending, when I stopped myself and instead wrote, "I'm grateful for our happy new beginning." For that is what this really feels like: a beginning. We're just getting started plumbing the depths, and the heights, of the sexual connection possible between us now—thanks to our enduring love and, I'm convinced, to our willingness to set each other free within the very context of our life as husband and wife.

We may not always live this way, with separate rooms, not meeting up most days until midday, often engaging in our own pursuits in the evenings, but right now, it's working well for us individually and for our union. Who can predict what lies ahead and how we will want or need to adapt and grow? I certainly cannot. The one thing I know for sure, though, is that before life is over for me, change will come many times, and I feel so very fortunate to have—at this moment—an amazing partner by my side with whom to navigate the big adventures inevitable in its wake.

CHAPTER 13

Two Peas in My Peace Pod

Having written a lot about love, it feels like time to address another important quality of being that's figured prominently in my healing journey. Earlier, I used the word *equanimity* to describe the underlying steadiness that has come into my life over these last years, but another—perhaps better, or at least more generally accessible—way to describe it would be to use the word *peace*. I suspect more people might be able to conjure up a sense from their own experience of what that state feels like. Unsurprisingly, I didn't inhabit it much in my first fifty-eight years of life, battered as I was by wild swings along the jagged line of stuck traumatic energy. Medication certainly tamed some of the wild fluctuation, but not in any curative way, simply blunting dysfunction. Only relatively recently have I embodied true peace more consistently, and, oddly enough, I have COVID and the general chaos of 2020 to thank for showing me how profoundly it has sunk in, how much of a core trait of mine it is now.

As the pandemic unfolded, with its seemingly endless concurrent social, political, and environmental tumults, I detected a stark difference between my response to it all and that of many other people—in my sphere and out in the wider world. I experienced the same fear, uncertainty, and sadness that I heard others express. But as the feelings arose, I'd welcome and explore them, and then they'd pass through me, and I'd gently settle back into a baseline of steadiness, even comfort with the unknown. I rode the many waves, while all around me, I saw people locking into states of anxiety or depression, with all the mental and physical anguish those states engender—in themselves and everyone around them. I saw people getting hijacked by their nervous system's danger response.

In September of 2020, wildfires ravaged outlying areas of the county where I live, filling the sky with smoke, darkening the days with a strange orange glow, and preventing us from venturing outdoors except when absolutely necessary. This crisis within a crisis further exacerbated pandemic-induced isolation by removing the soothing balm of being in nature. I watched myself take even that setback in stride and remain balanced, while a friend of mine who lives in the same area—equally distant from the fires, we were never in immediate danger—spun into terror, growing sick and sleepless with worry. When the skies eventually cleared and I could safely go outside again, I felt my spirits lift, alerting me that while my body and brain may have remained calm, my psyche must have suffered some—important to know. As fresh air filled my lungs, sunshine warmed my skin, and the blue of the sky soothed my eyes, I felt an immediate melting away of a sense of disconnection from the natural world I live in—ah, so that's what must have troubled my spirit—and a swift restoration of buoyancy. For my poor friend, however, it took days to recover from the exhaustion of her hyperarousal, to let go of and dig out from under the panic, dread, and fear she'd succumbed to.

I couldn't help but wonder, *What's different for me? Why do alarm and stress have such a hard time getting a grip on me and such an easy time with others?* I knew that the answer had to go beyond the obvious privileged bubble from which I've navigated these extraordinary times. It had to, because I'd seen folks who share similar circumstances to mine—financially secure, in good health, in a life-stage free of the challenges of parenting young children or caregiving elders—paralyzed by despair or consumed with anxiety, or both, over these long months of local, national, and global upheaval. In the end, I could only attribute the contrast in reaction and response to the somatic healing work I've had the great good fortune to undertake and the embodied peace that it has brought to me. My brain, in fact my entire nervous system, is radically different than it used to be, and its profound, permanent change accounts for my steadiness in the face of challenging circumstances, for my resilience.

Not long after the wildfires subsided, and I'd had that epiphany, this truth coalesced for me as I read Lissa Rankin's *Mind Over Medicine*. In it, she cites from Dawson Church's *Bliss Brain* the commonalities in mystical states of consciousness:

- Feeling of deep and profound peace
- Certainty that all things will work out for the good
- Sense of my own need to contribute to others
- Conviction that love is at the center of everything
- Sense of joy and laughter
- An experience of greater emotional intensity
- Great increase in my understanding and knowledge
- Sense of the unity of everything and my own part in it
- Sense of new life or living in the world
- Confidence in my own personal survival
- Feeling that I couldn't possibly describe what was happening to me

- The sense that the universe is alive
- The sensation that my personality has been taken over by something much more powerful than I am
- A sense of tremendous personal expansion, either psychological or physical

Reading what felt eerily like a portrait of my own baseline brain state laid out so systematically in writing startled me, especially when I realized I'd actually used some of the same words, self-descriptively, in my journaling and here in this book.

It hit me that I often hang out in "bliss brain," this list of states that for thousands of years wisdom teachers described and now contemporary scientists present as a sort of neurological map of robust mental health. It also might be called inner peace, and I inhabit it not just when I'm "in a trance" or having a "mystical experience," but much of the time in my daily reality. At first unnerved at realizing this fact, I soon relaxed into the embrace of inevitability. After all, I had been purposely using highly proven techniques—both ancient and modern—to accomplish just such a healing transformation, like millions of seekers over the millennia. The fact that my nervous system went from a mass of tangled, misfiring wires, broken links, and dead zones, wreaking perpetual havoc for almost six decades, to a more smoothly functioning network of fluid connections primed for well-being and growth is both mundane and miraculous. Something to both take in stride and stand in awe of, and to be deeply thankful for. Which brings me to the first of the two peas in my "peace pod": gratitude, its late appearance in this book perhaps belying its power and essential role in my healing.

It feels important to state that the tale of my transformation, from my defining moment on, is certainly not one of a total about-face from ungrateful wretch to pillar of thankfulness. I didn't start out as an unappreciative person, more like a partially unaware one, someone half-asleep to the true richness of her blessings. Becoming more fully conscious in this domain, like all the rest, began in 2017 with mindfulness and learning to meditate using my breath as an anchor. Somehow, by paying exquisite attention—over and over—to the experience of cool air passing through my nostrils, traveling down my throat, filling my lungs on the inhale, and then flowing back up and out, warm in my nostrils on the exhale, I encountered the gift of life itself. Intimately linked to awakening to privilege, I could no longer take even breathing for granted, and it felt like my eyes had snapped open suddenly to find a great floodlight illuminating beauty, love, and good fortune all around me, in great swaths and in the tiniest of details. I walked around with an unfamiliar fullness in my heart.

It was about this time that my son introduced me to the Greater Good Science Center (GGSC) at the University of California, Berkeley, which helped me put a name on this new feeling. According to GGSC's mission statement, it "studies the psychology, sociology, and neuroscience of well-being, and teaches skills that foster a thriving, resilient, and compassionate society." With one of their study and teaching focuses being gratitude, I now not only understood what I was feeling, but I also encountered scientific proof of how important it is to individual and collective happiness, health, and wholeness. In the face of their assertion that gratitude—with its power to transform personal lives and the lives of communities—can be nurtured through practice, I decided to dedicate some of my time and energy to its conscious cultivation. To take this lovely feeling and run with it.

I started with the idea of keeping a gratitude journal, and now, four years later, I'm still at it and have a hunch I'll never stop. Every evening, in the hour or so before bedtime, in the hushed quiet of a nearly dark house—or hotel room, or apartment, or wherever I am at the time—I always, with only rare exceptions, spend time by myself on this practice. I sit comfortably, take time to breathe deeply and quiet my mind and body, then open the notebook I keep on hand for this purpose alone. I think and feel back through my waking hours and record what I'm thankful for that day and why, in whatever form of list bubbles up from within me in that moment. When I first started this practice, unsure about it and still trapped in a lot of old pain, my gratitude lists were pretty basic—home, family, friends—and often repetitive, one day to the next. But over time, as I healed and became more comfortable with the practice itself, really leaning into it, my lists grew in variety and scope. Now, they often astonish me with their creativity or surprise me with their content.

Just the other day, I found myself entering a rather painful interpersonal experience at the top of my nightly log, not something one typically thinks of being grateful for. But as my pen flowed over the page and spilled forth the learning I'd found in the conflict, and the wisdom I'd gained from facing it, it was crystal clear why I'd chosen it. When I paused to take in the hard thing I'd just given thanks for, the phrase, "When you can be grateful for the crap, you've arrived," popped into my head. I don't know if this aphorism is attributable to someone, if I'd heard it somewhere before, or if it was just the fruit of my own brain at the time, but I understood its truth for me in a flash.

That flare of insight soon turned into a fit of mirth as the thought then came to me that I'd been grateful for crap—literally—for over three years. Ever since trauma therapy cured my chronic constipation, I have not taken for granted the smooth elimination of my body's solid waste—now, almost every morning like clockwork—in the slightest. Not after enduring over a half-century of struggle. In fact, sometimes early on in my healing, I would put my hand on my lower belly and whisper, "Thank you, dear body," as the movement slipped easily from me. It felt miraculous, almost holy. (Not the kind of experience everyone would find sacred or describe as having "arrived," I know, but I'm growing quite comfortable with being an outlier.)

Flexing my gratitude muscle with constant, purposeful repetition and watching it yield a new strength of character has been one of the easier pieces of growth I've undertaken. In fact, it has often brought pure delight to my frequently difficult journey, for which I feel very thankful. (See what happens?) It's an attitudinal shift rich with reward, which William Arthur Ward started to capture when he said, "Gratitude can transform common days into Thanksgivings, turn routine into joy, and change ordinary opportunities into blessings." In my experience, though, the positive effects extend way beyond the personal, where Ward seats it. Yes, the practice of gratitude first worked on me internally, but by so altering my very way of seeing, it also changed my way of being in the world, transforming all my relationships: with people closest to me, out in my community, in wider society, and even with the planet itself. The ripple effect has been tremendous and led me to think of the healing potential for the world.

I guess that's why in my further exploration of gratitude I next gravitated toward A Network for Grateful Living founded by Brother David Steindl-Rast, whom I quoted in my introduction. On the network's website, I found echoes of my own experience and thoughts in these words: "We hold grateful living as an engaged mindfulness practice, grounded in both wisdom and science, which supports our ability to see the wonder and opportunity in every moment, and motivates us to *act* [emphasis mine] boldly with love, generosity, and respect toward one another, ourselves, and the Earth." In other words, they believe that gratefulness is key to peace—inner peace and peace in the world. I do too.

Another essential ingredient in peace is forgiveness—the second pea in my pod. Many books have been written on the subject of forgiveness, often including formal practices designed to help the reader let go of their tight hold on grievances as a pathway to personal and relational healing. While I love that these resources exist, I never felt drawn to pick up any of them and wasn't sure why until very recently. I don't remember what prompted the insight, but one day not long ago, it dawned on me that my challenge with forgiveness had lain in a completely different direction. I had required an alternate kind of help, which I'd blessedly stumbled into through somatic work: I had needed to actually *claim* my grievances, since you can't let go of something you haven't first held onto.

By *claim*, I mean own their reality bodily. As I've mentioned before, over the many courses of talk therapy I'd undertaken throughout my years, I'd gained some awareness of troubling things that had happened in my life, ways people had hurt me, sins committed against me. I had also grappled with how I had hurt or harmed others. Together, these twin cognitive reckonings shifted my perspective and afforded me some much-needed mental relief, leading me to my earliest exercises in pardoning self and others. Through my foray into ACOA therapy, I came to understand that my mother's alcoholism had wounded me; to grasp the dynamics at play in her, the family, and me; and to absolve her in my mind. But then trauma recovery came along, revealing the biological nature—the hardwired neurological and embedded physiological reality—of both my wounds and the core sense of self that arose from them, and I realized that those first efforts of exoneration were only an anemic shadow of forgiveness. An attitude adjustment had pointed me in the right direction, but full liberation could only come about corporally.

I didn't purposefully set out on a quest for the freedom that forgiveness brings, though. It arose organically on the waves of

somatic healing, much like how compassion bubbled up naturally out of mindfulness. Each time I consciously dove into the
depths of my body to befriend an old hurt and unlock its energy,
the ride always brought me back up and out into release—a state
I'd feel physically, mentally, emotionally, and spiritually. Like
that time at Esalen when I worked with my hip problem. After
that amazing discharge, through conscious dance, of the frozen
agony from rape, the nagging pain in my joint disappeared,
my painful thoughts of self-recrimination ceased, my hot anger
transmuted to a quiet peace, and my heavy heart swelled with
the lightness of love. I was unbound, at least partially.

I say partially, because I've also learned that depending on the size
or significance of the wound, more than one intimate encounter with
its pain may be necessary. To jump too quickly to forgiveness is, at
best, to offer a lukewarm version thereof, containing only minimal
healing potential. At worst, it's a form of spiritual bypassing—an
attempt to avoid pain that blocks liberation and is actually harmful
to the self and others. Some transgressions, like rape, are just too big
for an easy loosening, and there's no rushing the process. I had to
revisit that particular rupture a few times before I found true freedom,
before I was able to claim it fully, work it through, and then let it go.
While that rapist's behavior will forever remain abhorrent to me, I
have purged my resentment toward him as a person. In working to
heal myself, I accepted the full ugliness of how our worlds collided,
and came to understand our mutual suffering. I have truly forgiven
my perpetrator.

While some crimes against me have taken more time and effort
than others to grasp and let go of, in the end, I have pardoned
even the most egregious acts against me that I have brought to
consciousness so far. And seemingly without even trying. Yes, I've
worked hard at personal healing, but I haven't had to force forgiveness. When my body undams, absolution freely flows out. When

I physically release my grievances, my heart fills with mercy. I come to the core of aliveness within me and meet my transgressors there—in our shared full humanity, in both our common inevitable woundedness and essential perfection. I condemn bad actions while releasing the actors.

This is also the way I've worked on forgiving myself for the wrongs I've done to others as well as the harm I've caused myself over the years. A few months ago, I had a wonderful opportunity to work on the latter of those two dynamics. Summoned to the dental lab that had been trying unsuccessfully to fix a crown for me and seated in their exam chair, I heard myself say to the technician, "I'm sorry for being such a difficult client."

"Oh, that's okay," he said. "I want you to be happy."

You might be wondering, *Where's the harm to yourself in this exchange? It's good to admit when you're wrong and to say you're sorry, right?* And I'd generally agree. Trouble is, in this instance—as in too many others in my life—I *hadn't* done anything wrong, and as soon as I got in my car after our brief encounter, it hit me: I had just taken responsibility for another person's wrongdoing and shouldered blame that didn't belong to me—yet again. I marveled at how that old automatic assumption that if something is not going well, it must be *my* fault had snuck up on me so readily, even after all the personal growth work I'd undertaken.

In this case, the technician had repeatedly made glaring mistakes in the construction of my crown, dragging what normally would have been a two-week process into several months of extra appointments, numerous iterations of temporary appliances, and fresh gum discomfort each time, frustrating both me and my dentist. Not only had I tolerated the ineptitude patiently—like a good martyr does—but I had essentially crawled on my belly to him in contrition as if I were the problem, when in fact it was his original workmanship that had failed prematurely, requiring a replacement only one year after it had been "permanently" cemented in. It was an all too familiar dynamic, this habit of self-abasement. Perhaps starting long ago with that childhood incident with Jeff and my mother, which damaged more than my sexuality, laying down as it did my idea that *I* was the one who had done something wrong, that *I* was worthless and rotten.

I may have purged much of that erroneous self-image, and its automatic appearance in an incident with a dental crown held only minor consequences for my well-being. But how easily the apology had slipped from my lips—three plus years into healing—sounded a great reminder of how growing into wholeness is an ongoing multilayered process, a lifetime's task. Much of the hardest healing work already done, in this recent case all I needed to do was dedicate a few minutes to recollecting the origins of that toxic self-image. Then it was easy to forgive myself for the self-blaming pattern's emergence in my present and to recommit to its continued transformation. I also celebrated the recognition that, because its hold on me is so slight now, it can no longer bring me grievous harm like in the past.

I've repeatedly found this kind of simple (though not always easy) inner work to have socially—not just personally—transformative power, and my ongoing interaction with this dental technician is a case in point. In the car before my next meeting with him, I paused briefly to set the intention of staying true to the sense of myself as worthy, good, and right that now resides in my core. I then entered the building, and only a few moments into the actual meeting—barely past the opening conversational niceties—he said, unprompted, "I'm really sorry this has been such a mess. I've never had an appliance fail like that before. Yours is the first one, and I feel bad after all you've been through."

I tried not to gape, because only a day earlier I'd said to my husband, "I'd just like him to apologize," though I hadn't really put any stock in that happening. But now, here it was. "Thanks," I said to him. "I appreciate that. It has been a long, drawn-out saga. And this thing being in the front of my mouth, I just want it to be solid."

Less than a week later, he delivered a completely satisfactory finished crown to my dentist so that I had my smile restored to me in full, and I'm convinced that swift product turnaround, as well as his stark attitudinal one, happened because I shifted something inside myself. Much of human communication transcends the words or gestures we use and is energetic in nature—invisible and inaudible, but fully detectable—and this is primarily what we respond to, even if we remain unaware of it. By doing my inner work, then setting that intention in the car and bringing a completely different vibe to bear at our second meeting, the technician couldn't help but respond to me differently. *I* approached *him* differently, altering the energy flow between us. The dynamic was cleaner, personal boundaries were in place, each of us could own what belonged to us. All because I showed up to our interpersonal transaction in a more conscious way.

And there's the crux of it: consciousness. Merriam-Webster defines *consciousness* first as "the quality or state of being aware especially of something within oneself," and it lies at the core of my whole journey. It deserves its own chapter, certainly, and I will go there next. Before I do, I wish to circle back to where I started this one. The dual gifts of gratitude and forgiveness—those two marvelous peas in my peace pod—have undeniably helped me become conscious, wake up from a deep slumber, come to know myself more intimately, see the world profoundly differently, and inhabit life more easefully. In essence, to find peace— something that seems vitally important in light of today's chaotic reality, COVID and all. Dutch author and Holocaust victim Etty Hillesum said, "Ultimately, we have just one moral duty: to reclaim large areas of peace in ourselves, more and more peace, and to reflect it toward others. And the more peace there is in us, the more peace there will also be in our troubled world." I think she was on to something there. No, I know she was.

CHAPTER 14

⌒

Present Consciousness:
Transforming the Past, Shaping the Future

It's all very well and good for me to claim that consciousness is at the core of my healing journey, and I hope that by now I've painted a vivid enough picture to illustrate the truth of that understanding. It's yet another thing to assert that we are being called collectively to transform our very consciousness in order to face the challenges in our world—viral pandemic, environmental degradation, racial injustice, and more. What do I mean by that statement exactly? I'm not entirely sure. This idea represents new territory for me, some of it felt as truth on the visceral level yet still solidifying intellectually, some of it transcending my powers of expression, all of it mysterious. But so important I'm compelled to stretch myself beyond what I feel comfortable with and sure of. I invite you to come along with me on this thought experiment. (Or you could skip to the next chapter if you'd rather return to the nuts and bolts of healing. Feel free.)

Throughout these pages, I've talked a lot about what waking up—getting conscious—has meant for me. About how it has been a process of turning off automatic pilot and assuming the controls of my life, just as an actual aviator does when flight circumstances or safety concerns warrant. Autopilot represents the part of our mind operating outside of conscious perception, that is, below the level of our awareness, and is the state in which most of us spend much of our time. Scientific estimates for just how much time run as high as 95 percent of our waking hours. Trouble is, as science also tells us, many of the programs, assumptions, and information stores in this part of our mind were laid down early in life—during the first seven years, in fact—and so the vast majority of them (commonly up to 70 percent) are self-sabotaging, unsupportive, or negatively biased. Wow. Ponder the implications of that reality: until I was fifty-eight, without even knowing it, my thinking was that of a three-, five-, or seven-year-old. (Even well past fifty-eight. Witness the apology incident from the last chapter—proof of how powerfully persistent that early programming is.)

And it appears that this outcome is unavoidable—for each and every one of us. It's built right into *Homo sapiens* because we're born with brains still forming, and we're raised by human beings. You can take the idea of trauma out of it, if that concept doesn't resonate with you, but even if you were reared by basically good people with relatively healthy emotional lives (lucky you), they did not execute their roles flawlessly. They couldn't have because there's no such thing as a perfect person. Regardless of the level of health of your primary caregiver(s) at the beginning of your life, it's pretty much a guarantee that you did not get all your needs met, you received some harmful messages, and you internalized an at least partially inaccurate self-image.

I mean no disrespect to your parent(s) or caregiver(s), or mine, or anyone's. As if looking with clear sight is ever anything but holy, I've had various people raise the biblical injunction of "honor thy father and mother" with me as an argument against going back into one's past with a critical eye. I find this ironic because it was this very healing journey of mine that led me to value my parents more than ever before. By plumbing the depths of my own pain and how it lived in my body, I came face-to-face with their pain and how it lived in their bodies. In fully comprehending how early childhood experiences shape physiology, self-perception, and behaviors, I could now understand my father's toxic narcissism as an all but inevitable outcome of the abandonment of the family by his own father when mine was a very young child, his ensuing experiences of homelessness and hunger, and the chaos of his mother's repeated total mental breakdowns. Or my mother's ineluctable addictions as the almost unavoidable consequence of emotional abandonment by her mother, her family's refusal on religious grounds to medically treat her crippling spinal condition, and her father's untimely death, on top of the grinding oppression of her person by the patriarchal structures of her era. The incidents and events of their lives I just delineated are only the tip of the iceberg of trauma they each endured.

Through my process, my mother and father have become fully human to me, and fully heroic. Both survived circumstances and environments that bore the potential to destroy. They dragged scarred self-concepts and twisted relationship models into their marriage, and yet the home life they created for my sister and me, while unavoidably fraught with pain because neither of them ever woke to, nor sought to heal, their own wounds, was surprisingly warm and stable. That two such damaged souls could create a family where moments of fun, love, and care shined through as much as they did amidst the prevalent darkness is a testimony, I think, to the human spirit's ability to triumph over adversity and the heart's desire to make things better. I wouldn't have wanted to grow up in either of their childhood households, and I'm grateful to them for all they were able to give me despite their own devastating struggles. I honor my mother and father—all my ancestors—by looking at and freeing myself from my past, our shared past. In fact, I honor them in perhaps the deepest way possible by saying, "It ends here. In your name and mine, I will not pass on our pain any further."

To not go deep and do this work is a missed opportunity to both live one's true life to the fullest and to participate in healing the world—one I nearly passed up myself. I understand what can get in the way, I really do—from direct personal experience—and I have tremendous empathy and compassion for anyone on the precipice who feels daunted by the leap, especially those of us who find ourselves at a more advanced age. We can suffer from the inertia of too much time gone by, from the trap of well-worn behavioral and mental grooves that feel oh so comfortable, from bondage to the cultural view that there's something almost taboo or shameful about someone in their fifties, sixties, seventies "still" looking back at their childhood. To the one who says to me, "That was so long ago, it can't have any bearing on my life now," I say, "It has every bearing, because of how we're wired as a species." Or to the one who says, "I'm an adult, for heaven's sake," I say "Not really. Not until you do this work, because your child self is essentially still running the show." And finally, to the one who says, "I should have gotten over that by now," I say, "Well, you haven't, and in fact, you can't unless you bring it to consciousness and work it through the body." To us all, myself included, I say "Wishing does not make it so."

What's going on in the life of a dear friend of mine is a perfect example of what I'm talking about. Janice is a longtime committed meditator, cares about personal growth and well-being, and has benefited from a few courses of talk therapy over the years. An avid exerciser all her life, she has a super clean diet and lives a decidedly healthy lifestyle. All this, and she just recently received the stunning diagnosis of heart disease. On the surface, it seemed to make no sense whatsoever, until she went deeper. Aware of my full story, she reached out to me for support, specifically because of my trauma recovery experience. We'd talked in the past about how her periodic bouts of hives—an autoimmune disease—and ulcerative colitis, could have their roots in childhood trauma, but she'd not pursued that avenue of healing, the two conditions being easy to minimize in her mind perhaps because of their infrequent occurrences. But this was different; this was about a chronic and life-threatening condition. She felt like she'd had her wake-up call and wanted to talk to me about it.

On a walk together one day, she told me that she now knew in her gut that her health issues over the years, and probably this new problem, were likely due in large part to a difficult early child-hood and her ensuing sixty plus years of living with a dysregulated nervous system. She couldn't ignore the implications any longer, but despite this strong inner sense, she still felt reluctant to add somatic trauma therapy to her treatment plan. She expressed her struggle to me this way, "If I open up the past and get into my feelings, I'll never make it back out. I'm afraid of falling apart." I understand that fear, but the irony is that by not looking at her wounding and getting into her emotions somatically, she essen-tially consigns herself to the very thing she fears. Beneath the load of undischarged traumatic energy, her body is literally falling apart, quitting prematurely. One could almost say she's dying of a broken heart.

As I see it—and have experienced firsthand—going to pieces is good, essential even. The self I inhabited—knew well and lived as for six decades—was a false one, created as a survival mechanism in the face of other people's unresolved pain. Shattering that counter-feit self enabled me to recover my core elements and put them back together in a truer, more life-affirming way. Having fallen apart, I'm now, finally, truly me. As someone who has had a front row seat during my journey, Janice has witnessed and helped celebrate that very movement—the smashing apart and the reconfiguring into a shining greater wholeness. She has beheld, in person, the profound blessings I have written about in this book.

But seeing it in me and believing it about herself are two different things. On an intellectual level, she gets it, she's on board. But many factors conspire against her embracing it more fully at this point, among them cultural conditioning that denies the life-giving importance of emotions—especially "negative" ones—and a lack of trust in life that is often a legacy of trauma. Moving from theory into practice feels to Janice like a huge challenge. One she's not sure she's up for. I understand that. Time will tell what she chooses, and I will hold her close and support her no matter what, but you can imagine what my wish is for her.

Janice is not the only person I've found myself walking a delicate line with—between understanding and impatience. Because of my direct experience, it seems quite obvious to me now that the one great task of "growing up" is to face the truth that we are inevitably warped by our early experiences and to assume responsibility for our lives as adults by consciously reshaping ourselves, at whatever age we come to the work. To cling to the myth of benignity bizarrely surrounding childhood, or to ignore the need to look back and heal, is to remain in opposition to the basic facts of human existence and to choose—consciously or unconsciously— to stay stuck at a certain level of immaturity. I find myself wondering, *Why would any adult want to live with their young child's brain programming in control most of the time?* Put that way, I don't think anyone would.

But that's exactly what I was doing before my turning point and may be how the vast majority of people conduct their lives— cradle to grave—precisely because this fundamental truth is not talked about in modern Western culture, at least in the United States when I was growing up. Doesn't it seem like it ought to be? We shouldn't have to stumble upon it in the midst of crisis like I— and countless others—did. Our society would be radically altered, for the better I maintain, by open acceptance of our full humanity, and frank discussion of it from the very start of each life.

Off the top of my head, I can begin to imagine how differently the years of adolescence could look, how much less tumultuous they could be than the ones I spent engaging in self-harming behaviors like drinking and sexual promiscuity—all that rebellion simply a misguided, or rather, *un*guided, effort to "grow up." What if we were to actually encourage young people, as a part of their holy task of maturation at that important life phase, to throw off the crap we (the adults in their lives—parents, teachers, coaches, religious leaders) inevitably though inadvertently lay on them? And showed them how to do it? Over time, the need for even that intense work might diminish as the ensuing generations of more awake, fully integrated people turned toward becoming conscious parents.

I've seen how my life is transforming as I lift my subconscious beliefs into consciousness and physically alter them, and I've observed the positive ripple effects the energetic shift wrought by that personal process is having on those around me. What if I had been empowered to make this shift earlier? How much less pain would I have wrought on others, how much more of a positive force for good could I have been? What would our world be like if more cultures embraced the wisdom buried in our full species name— *Homo sapiens sapiens*: the animal that knows, and knows that it knows—and bravely raised children into full awareness, which has to include an embracing of their own personal power and an understanding of the shortcomings of the adults in their lives?

I've even had the thought that the continuation of human life on this Earth depends upon it. The unfortunately common story of never growing up—of allowing the subconscious to remain unexamined and unhealed—is not just a matter of personal tragedy; it bears tremendous social significance because of the very nature of existence itself. Late nineteenth-century thinker William James said, "We are like islands in the sea, separate on the surface but connected in the deep," and contemporary science has proven just how profoundly true that statement is. Findings from fields as diverse as neurology, evolutionary biology, and quantum physics point sharply away from the reductionist, materialist view that has dominated popular thinking for centuries and compellingly toward the fundamental interconnectedness of all life and a living-systems orientation for understanding our world.

To bring this lofty thought down to the personal level, I take this to mean that how I show up in life has impact not only for myself, but for those around me, and ultimately, far beyond me. So, I ask myself: *What do I want to put out into our system? What kind of energy do I want to add to the collective field?* I feel almost giddy about the power open to me—to all of us—to make a positive difference in the world through the truth of our interconnectedness. On the flip side of that glee lies a more sober sense of responsibility to not contribute unconscious woundedness to the world. As Jiddu Krishnamurti said, "What you are, the world is. And without your transformation, there can be no transformation of the world." This perspective wipes out the right to look out at the ills of the world and point fingers at others. It smashes the illusion that any of us are exempt from accountability for the state of the whole.

This point seems particularly poignant in the wake of Donald Trump's presidency. On perhaps the most public stage available on our globe, the man strikingly personified absolute unconscious woundedness and exposed the far-reaching lethal toxicity of that state for all the world to see and feel. As he vacillated between behaviors more appropriate to a petulant toddler or an elementary school bully than to a mature adult, it was so very clear that he has never undertaken the essential work of growing up—of looking back at his painful (clearly traumatic) past, of bringing his deep sense of unworthiness into the light of awareness, and of reprogramming his early-formed subconscious beliefs.

While I detest the catastrophic suffering that Donald Trump engendered on individual and social levels, I also believe he was a great gift to our nation, maybe even to the world, because he held up an enormous crystal-clear mirror that we couldn't help but look into. He provided a magnified reflection of the sickness of our American culture and—hopefully—a wake-up call. He was a potent, larger than life example of why personal healing work is vitally important to the world. Anyone who criticizes our forty-fifth president without also looking inward to find where similar old pain resides in themselves and undertaking the work to transmute it simply contributes their own unconscious wounding and subconscious programming to the power of his deeply harmful energetic field.

I didn't vote for Donald Trump, but because I'm part of the collective, I cannot completely absolve myself from responsibility for his ascendancy. That would be to ignore my interconnectedness with the whole. I find myself wondering about the ways in which old patterns of mine might have rippled out to help create the disenfranchisement that elected him, especially since my conscious awakening didn't begin until after his inauguration. I also find myself feeling grateful for the gift of awareness that has come to me since then and remain committed to continuing to grow in it. I can't expect to effectively do the work of social transformation that so desperately needs to be done by all of us without first—and continually—doing my own inner work. In speaking about the work of liberation for all, author, poet, and activist Alice

Walker urges people to start with themselves first and only then to move toward helping the other—an approach to the task I readily embrace and hope more people will join in.

Other than adding positive energy to the collective field—which is always good—I'm not sure that my hope is much of a factor here. Because I see signs all over that this shift is happening despite ourselves. Take one tiny step away from the mainstream profit-oriented media that is in thrall to our current toxic cultural paradigm and there is overwhelming evidence of a vast groundswell movement linking personal responsibility and planetary healing. Off the top of my head, the following organizations and individuals come to mind: Education for Racial Equity, the Mind & Life Institute, Vote With Love, Spring Washam, the Embodiment Conference, TreeSisters, Commune, Thomas Hübl, the Fetzer Institute, Joanna Macy, the Center for Mind-Body Medicine, the Consciousness and Healing Initiative, the HeartMath Institute, Science and Nonduality, Gabor Maté, the Revolutionary Love Project. These are just a smattering of the countless individuals, events, and organizations out there leading the way. I may have just recently opened my mind, but many others have been speaking from this understanding long before me, and my joining their ranks feels inevitable. Not so much something I did, but a way life moved me.

The idea that the state of our individual consciousness matters to the world is grounded in ancient wisdom, has been transmitted in myriad ways throughout the ages, and is now being confirmed by modern science and refined by contemporary thinkers. It is gaining powerful traction in the urgency of our time, and I'm being pulled along on the energy of a tide much larger than I. As a lifelong open-water swimmer, I know the key to survival in a strong current is to relax and go with it—I may be ushered somewhere unplanned, but I will eventually come out safely. If I fight against it, I'll only exhaust myself and risk drowning.

I'm applying this same wisdom to living at this extraordinary evolutionary moment. I'm choosing to lean into the flow of life, into universal consciousness (perhaps the ultimate embodiment of Love?) completely unsure of where it'll take me but trusting the ride, nonetheless. I need to live my life in such a way that, should I be lucky enough to get to reflect on it at the end, I will be able to say, "It may have taken me a long time to get down to it, but I embraced the essential work of being human: of knowing and knowing that I know—of getting conscious and growing up. And by so engaging, I helped make the world a better place."

I already see the proof of that claim in the ways my personal transformation has touched the lives of family members, friends, and people in my various communities in positive ways. The breathtakingly brief time left to me here in this life—however long that proves to be—will most likely not permit me to glimpse similar "results" in wider realms, never mind on the global level, but I'm taking the long view. As Native American and other Indigenous cultures have always known, I must live in the present for the benefit of future generations.

CHAPTER 15

Odds and Ends

I have a growing sense that my work here is winding down, that I'm coming to the end of this book. I've certainly not arrived at the end of my healing journey, but I see that the first two phases of it are completing, providing a natural place to take a break from the hard work of putting it into words. To borrow imagery from my therapist Gloria's I AM The Medicine healing model, the years I've depicted here represent mainly a vast thawing from trauma, a languid floating in the element of water where I have moved from generalized fear into a deep trust in life and found myself and my purpose. Followed by entry into the realm of the element of wood where, like the sap that feeds the growth of a tree, embracing anger brought me clarity about my needs, taught me to stand up for them, and fueled my creativity. Moving into a new phase now, my heart broken wide open, my task is learning the right use of the power of love I found there. I've entered that realm of the element of fire, and I yearn to be a good steward—not to simply smolder, nor generate an inferno, but to burn with a steady warmth for myself and others to bask in. I have much to learn.

This shift is too new for me to write about extensively. I need to dedicate myself to living it before I try to reflect on it. Perhaps later, when I've had a chance to look back from wherever this phase will take me, I'll be moved to write a second book about my journey. Or perhaps not. In any case, it seems like a good time for us to part ways for now. Before I wrap this whole thing up, though, I'd like to mention a few additional tools that have been essential to my joyous overhaul thus far. One or more of them just might resonate with you and help you with yours, should you decide to embark on such an undertaking. Each of these subjects is a pearl of great beauty, deserving of close examination and worthy of volumes of words, but given the scope of this project, a few paragraphs about each will have to suffice.

Maybe it'll come as no surprise that nature has played a key role in my restoration. Over human history, so many other people—authors, poets, songwriters, philosophers, physicians, mystics—have spoken to this truth, of how being out in the wide, wild world is a salve to the soul, a balm to the nervous system. I must add my voice to this chorus. During these past few tumultuous years, spending time in the woods, at a local park, by the ocean, in the mountains, at an arboretum, even in my own tiny backyard—anywhere nature is alive and present—has brought the kind of solace and inspiration that only being immersed in the power, beauty, and timelessness of something far greater than the self can. It has offered me a wider perspective. Soaking in the sights and smells and sounds and feels—even tastes, if I am careful—of the great outdoors renews my senses, helps me stay in the present moment and reminds me that I am part of the web of life. All good things to remember on the healing journey, perhaps on any journey.

Plus, Mother Nature is the greatest teacher on the cyclic character of existence. After almost every therapy session with Gloria, I visit the beach in the town where her office is located. Even just a few minutes of watching the rolling blue-gray waves of the Pacific crashing on shore and then receding—over and over—soothingly reminds me of life's unending rhythms and that those same movements are present in me. Nature also instructs brilliantly about impermanence. When I visit the same place repeatedly and take in how different it is each time, it helps me recall that everything changes. Everything passes away. New things always arise. That's just how life works, and it lies beyond my control. There's true liberation in that realization, which helps me relax into the inevitability of change in my own life.

Lastly, getting back in touch—literally—with nature has helped me become more whole. I discovered the power of a tactile relationship with our planet through the practice of grounding, otherwise known as earthing. There was a time between therapy sessions about a year into my personal trauma recovery process where I hit a healing crisis that brought on a cluster of intense physical symptoms—room-spinning vertigo, body-engulfing nausea, and bone-crushing fatigue—with alarming suddenness, and quelling them required quite a bit of extra TLC. When I reached out to Gloria for support, part of her "first-aid" prescription for me was to go outside and stand on the ground in my bare feet for twenty minutes at a time, three to four times a day, for the next few days, preferably near a tree. Earlier in my life, I would have scoffed at such a suggestion, but having journeyed with Gloria for some time and come into such a beautiful new place in my life, I readily gave it a try. Its effectiveness stunned me.

Postcrisis, when my intellectual curiosity returned, I asked her about the specific healing mechanism involved. I had to know what was going on. Why did her barefoot prescription help me feel so much better? How it works is pretty simple, really, and is once again something Indigenous cultures have known since time immemorial, and modern science is just now leading us back to. Humans are bioelectric organisms meant to exist in direct contact with Earth's electric energy. Unfortunately, industrialized society—with its "advancements" like synthetic-soled shoes and living predominantly indoors—has essentially severed that connection, with deleterious effect. By standing in my bare feet in my yard, I reconnected to the planet I live on. I plugged into its beneficial negative charge to counter the positive overcharge that had built up in me—I physically grounded myself, in the exact same way the electrical system of my house is grounded for proper functioning. When my skin meets the ocean or any of Earth's natural waters, I derive the same benefit.

Like a good nerd, I've done a lot of research since that episode and conducted my own personal experiments. What I've come to is this: I am meant to live body-to-body with my home world, and I now build in that direct contact in as many ways as I can, reveling in the improved mental and physical health it brings. When paths and trails allow, I walk and hike in bare feet, my soles pawing Earth's top layer; as much as possible (without courting hypothermia), I forgo a wetsuit when I swim, welcoming the ocean's feel on my skin; I lie directly on the sand for part of my time at the beach, nestling into a hollow where every cell on my surface contacts a grain of our home planet's. Oh, and for good measure, I hug trees, caress rocks, and touch plants I know are safe.

I've noticed that sometimes what I do causes people to look twice, but I don't care. It matters not to me what they may be thinking—good, bad, or neutral. Occasionally, instead of just gaping, someone will inquire about my activity and its motivations, and I happily share my findings, thoughts, and resources. Just the other day, I saw one such previous questioner walking barefoot in the distance, along a route she had stopped me on months ago. I had to smile because she had told me originally that even though she understood the benefits, she was too self-conscious to do what

I was doing. Celebrating that she had obviously chucked that internal impediment to well-being, I sent a silent cheer of *Brava!* in her direction.

Along with a deep thank you to Mother Nature for her assistance in my healing, I also must offer profound gratitude to India, both ancient and modern, for the invaluable wisdom gifts of Ayurveda and yoga nidra. Both have influenced me in significant ways. Loosely translated, the word *Ayurveda* means "science of life" and refers to an understanding of human health—a medical system—that is five thousand years old. I stumbled upon it similarly to the way I bumped into 5Rhythms, while exploring something else entirely. I don't even remember what free online educational summit I was sampling at the time, but I found myself drawn to a presentation by world-respected Ayurvedic practitioner and teacher Acharya Shunya, attracted by both her photograph and the synopsis she'd provided about her upcoming talk.

Her hour did not disappoint, and I grew intrigued, wanting to learn more. I read her book *Ayurveda Lifestyle Wisdom* next and then explored various online resources, and eventually came across the Chopra Center's offerings on the subject. I find so much about Ayurveda remarkable that I struggle to know what exactly to share here, but for the sake of concision, I'll sum it up like this: I *met* myself there. The system accounted for things as disparate as my premature gray hair and my seasonal health challenges in a completely matter-of-fact way, no pathologizing whatsoever, providing a welcome haven not long after I'd permanently escaped my allopathic nightmare. Wanting to avail myself of its benefits more directly, I discovered a wonderful Ayurveda practitioner in my area, Nina Shah, and with her guidance, I'm learning how to adapt my diet and lifestyle to the various rhythms of nature in ways that help balance my unique system.

Another gift India has given me is yoga nidra, which is different from what many in the West associate with the word *yoga* as it does not involve poses, or asanas. Essentially, it's an ancient practice of profound relaxation that takes you to a kind of deep yet conscious sleep. Studies have shown that, like mindfulness meditation, it can help you access theta brainwaves—calming the sympathetic nervous system and leading to a host of benefits like increased immunity, improved digestion, or better stress management. Studies have also indicated that yoga nidra can take you beyond that state, into the realm of delta brainwaves—the slowest the human brain generates—where vital mental and physical renewal occurs, mainly through activation of the pineal gland. Modern science simply confirms what the ancients understood intuitively about this powerful body-mind-spirit practice. Karen Brody, creator of Daring to Rest, a yoga nidra methodology centered on rest and women's leadership, calls it "lying down to wake up," and I can testify that it feels delicious—during and after.

Since yoga nidra comprises several essential parts and requires skilled guidance to practice, I'm thankful that there are expert practitioners who have made it their life's work to bring this somewhat esoteric science to a broad lay audience. People like Karen Brody as well as Tracee Stanley (Radiant Rest) and Richard Miller (iRest) to name just three here in the West. These folks share a passion for the power of this medicine and a desire to make it accessible to all. With their resources, all you need is a smart phone or computer, any place to get comfortable, and maybe some earbuds, and profound restoration is at hand. Partly because it's geared specifically to empowering women, Daring to Rest has been a favorite of mine, playing a vital role in fostering my quest to reclaim the feminine power that is my birthright yet lay so long stifled within me. I offer a deep bow to Karen Brody for her work.

When I first began my exploration of yoga nidra in 2019, I did the forty-day program as outlined in Brody's eponymous book *Daring to Rest*, and it would be hard to overstate its positive impact on my well-being. Most salient to that time in my life was how much my practice of yoga nidra during the day helped my nights. I was going through my first fall without medication and struggling with some sleep disturbance, having trouble both falling and staying asleep, which was taking a toll on my energy level and mood. I don't even remember how I found the resource of yoga nidra, but after only a week of consistent daily practice, that frustrating insomniac groove began to shift. Not long thereafter, I locked into a blessed pattern of enjoying a full seven to eight hours of deep, lovely, much-needed sleep every night, with only rare exceptions.

Early on in my yoga nidra exploration, when I read Karen's bonus instructional booklet encouraging her students to create for themselves what she calls a yoga nidra rest cave as a way to support consistent practice, I knew I'd found someone simpatico. And this brings me to the final odd bit I want to share.

Almost two years before my first encounter with yoga nidra, at the very start of my healing journey, I had adopted a tiny spare bedroom in my house as a place to meditate, and spontaneously dubbed it the Bat Cave. Originally, I assumed the name must have come up out of ancient memories of watching the campy live-action TV show *Batman* during my childhood, because I've never read the comic books nor seen any of the movies made over the years. And I figured it had popped into my head because it was always dark in there when I dragged myself to it in the early morning. On further reflection, it's clear to me that the name came from a place more mystical than that, from the realm of archetypes perhaps, because it became a safe space that held my secrets, where I could be truly who I was, and where I went to transform myself, just like the character Bruce Wayne did.

I wish I'd taken periodic photos of the Bat Cave over these four years, because it has changed radically, right alongside me, providing a perfect reflection of what I've undergone within its shelter. At first, I hauled in an unused comfy chair and plopped it in the mess the room had become over the years as the catchall place to put things we weren't sure what to do with. For lack of a better spot, I set the chair in the room-wide closet, which gaped open because we had removed the doors long ago in a futile effort to make a small area larger and more functional. I shared space with a broken lamp, old CD racks, a pile of spare bedding we used for company, and random small pieces of no longer used but not yet discarded furniture. Stained dingy carpet that smelled like old dog, one lone overhead light fixture, and a window view of a blank wall rounded out the picture, but, my God, it was beautiful to me because it was mine.

Over the years, I've dropped the *bat* and now simply call it the Cave, because it has come to represent so much more to me than it originally did. I don't just meditate in it. It's also where I write, dance, do yoga nidra and various other self-care and spiritual practices, and where I house my library of resources for the journey— all the books and articles that have enlightened and guided me, and the journals that have accompanied me. It is also home to an altar of sorts that I've created from treasures I've collected in nature or been gifted with, and that changes over time as I shift and grow. At this very moment, I'm typing on my laptop at an inviting desk I built into the very closet I just described, which now sports handsome doors I can open and close as I wish. Lovely artwork adorns the soft green walls, cushy new carpet caresses my toes, and lush potted plantings and a precious peacock wall sculpture gifted to me by my son now fill the view from my window. It's my favorite room in the house, my sanctuary.

In many ways, the transformation of the Cave resembled mine: both gradual and nearly total, filled with serendipity yet subject to setbacks, unplanned but so very welcome. I'm not sure I could have accomplished my own transformation as freely without the Cave's empowering haven. I have never once taken for granted my great good fortune of having extra living space, never mind that I can claim it for my sole use. I often felt encouraged and prodded on by the idea attributed to Virginia Woolf that a woman should have a room of her own. Imagine my surprise when just recently I discovered that her feminist essay published in 1929 entitled "A Room of One's Own"—a piece I'd heard of but hadn't actually read—was specifically about women writers. Well, what do you know? And here I am.

I'm reminded of something my Feldenkrais teacher is fond of saying, because it underlies that body of work: "Everything is connected." Her phrase refers specifically to human physiology but also to founder Moshé Feldenkrais's broader understanding: in every moment we're alive, we are thinking, moving, sensing, and feeling, and it's *all* related. This truth of interconnectivity applies not just to direct human experience, but also to life across the board. It certainly has in my own healing story. Just now, as I was writing about the role of yoga nidra in easing my insomnia, keen awareness hovered in my brain of the changes that were simultaneously occurring in me through somatic therapy and Ayurveda at that time. I cannot simply pin it—or any of my "cures"—on one factor. The interrelatedness of the individual elements creates the reality, and the beauty, of the whole.

This multiyear odyssey of reclaiming my well-being resembles an intricate tapestry: pull one thread, and it tugs on the entire piece; leave one strand out, and the pattern is incomplete. Even the writing of this book figures into the healing. By using a kind of internal magnifying glass to examine piece by piece the images of these events, changes, challenges, and learnings, by picking apart the threads and following where they led, I've unexpectedly come to a far greater understanding of myself, other people, my relationships—of the entire journey so far. Like Florida Scott-Maxwell wrote, "You need only claim the events of your life to make yourself yours. When you truly possess all you have been and done, which may take some time, you are fierce with reality."

I'm struck by how similar this process has been to how I always approach viewing an impressionist painting when at a museum. I start by standing back and taking in the whole image, savoring the composition and overall beauty, the mood, the quality of light. Then I slowly draw nearer and nearer and watch with fascination as the image gradually dissolves into nothing more than individual brushstrokes. I love to peer closely at and get lost in the textures, colors, and movement of the often-great gobs of paint, the concrete reality of the piece. Eventually, though, I tire of such focused examination of the details, and as now with this book, I feel called to step back again, to look upon the lovely whole one last time, and to commence traveling toward the next treasure that lies in store for me.

CONCLUSION

It always comes back to the same necessity: go deep enough
and there is a bedrock of truth, however hard.
—*May Sarton*

Whew! Just as Brother David Steindl-Rast predicted, with nowhere to travel, go deep I did in writing this book during the COVID-19 quarantine. How uncanny that in the days of winding it down I should encounter the above quote from Sarton, because she absolutely nails the essence of my experience. I did indeed get down to the bedrock of truth, and facing and writing about some of it was exceedingly hard. But much of it was also unexpectedly delightful. That's because hardness doesn't constitute bedrock's only important quality. Merriam-Webster defines *bedrock* as "the solid rock underlying the soil and other unconsolidated materials . . . , lowest point, nadir . . . , basis, foundation." While writing this book, just as during the whole of my healing journey, I diligently excavated to my lowest point, shoveling aside the broken and weathered regolith of my life to find my personal bedrock—my essential unbrokenness, the solid foundation of who I am, my fundamental self—and I discovered some pretty wonderful things under the awful. As anyone would, I believe, if only they dare to look.

That's the thing any healing journey requires—looking. Taking in the whole picture and all its details. If I had never dared to peer at the ugly and the painful in my life, I wouldn't have found the astonishingly beautiful and the utterly redeeming. On the other side—for the most part—of wading into and mucking about in the difficult darkness, I now see that there is also great benefit in spending time gazing at the lovely light, for it is just as important, just as true. So, while I might have started out with Seane Corn's assertion that "Your pain is your purpose" as my motivator, I have shifted perspective somewhat. Pain might have pushed me at first, but now pleasure pulls me. Instead of fixating solely on what needs transformation, I also purposefully concentrate on celebrating what works and on staying open to the bliss that is here now, to the blessings of embodying post-traumatic growth.

I tacked a quote from author, philosopher, theologian, educator, and civil rights leader Howard Thurman in pride of place above my desk, and I reread it frequently. Its words sum up how I want to be on purpose in this final phase of life, in these, my crone, years. He said, "Don't ask what the world needs. Ask what makes you come alive and go do it. Because what the world needs is people who have come alive." True now more than ever it seems, and since writing and dancing make me come alive—and thrive—going forward, they are two ways I'll endeavor to serve this wounded and wonderful world. A third way will be through learning, precisely what led me to the other two in the first place. Along the path of healing, I've come to know and to esteem my intense curiosity. I never feel happier, more excited, and alive, than when I'm exploring new territory—of the mind, the body, the spirit—and I plan to keep that up until my dying breath, life willing.

When I take the time—maybe in a couple years—to reread this book, I hope that in some places I'll laugh to myself and say, "I can't believe I ever thought that." Because that will mean I have continued to grow, to ask why, and to have come to new understandings of myself, our existence, the Universe. Malcolm Gladwell got it right when he said, "That's your responsibility as a person, as a human being—to constantly be updating your positions on as many things as possible. And if you don't contradict yourself on a regular basis, then you're not thinking." I aspire to contradict myself regularly, for the rest of my days. After all, change is the only constant in life.

There was perhaps no better reminder of that truth than the landscape that surrounded me in Lone Pine. During the many moments I spent gazing at the soaring, jagged peaks of the gray granite Eastern Sierras (instead of my laptop), they seemed to my eye like something eternal, unmoving. But the fact is they have been constantly morphing—subject to uplift, glaciation, shifting plates, volcanic activity—for millions of years. While the pace of change for something as massive as a mountain range is infinitesimally slow—the current uplift rate of the Sierras is one to two millimeters per year, though this is deemed rapid in geological terms—the pace of change is much faster for us humans, for tiny-in-comparison me, and I feel that truth acutely.

In fact, I have this vague sense that I'm already sailing beyond some of what I've written here in these pages, though I wholeheartedly stand by it all. I can't exactly explain the feeling, but it has something to do with the current of life—the conscious evolutionary forces that I mused on in chapter 14—sweeping all of us along: an enormously hopeful groundswell, a broad deep undulation of healing ushered in by the seismic disturbances of the pandemic, climate change, social unrest. Despite believing that things will necessarily get more tumultuous before they get meaningfully better—think of the caterpillar destroyed to become the butterfly, of my shattering to become more whole—I'm buoyed by optimism. I look around me and see so many signs that positive change is underway; for example, the defeat of Donald Trump at the US polls in November 2020.

As one of the dancers in my 5R community so eloquently put it when we gathered online the Sunday following Election Day, "The great hate experiment failed, and now we get to try the great love experiment." I don't know this woman or her partner intimately, but I have danced many hours and participated in many sharing circles with them, and I feel great affection and admiration for both. They are at least two decades younger than I—I'm guessing—and exemplify part of why I'm so hopeful about the future. One appears quiet and reserved, the other outgoing and vivacious; both seem to me to be deep wells, unafraid to think, be, act, dress differently than the mainstream, unabashed in their passion for one another and for social justice, so much more comfortable with the fluidity of life than those in my generation who like to cling to the safety of clear-cut dualities. I look forward to the day when younger people like these two are fully in charge of our world.

Before I draw this book to a close, I'd like to return to where I began it—to hair. A year and a half has passed since I first sat down to write—having found inspiration in gray roots—and much has happened in that time. One of the developments that I celebrate is the resounding "Hell, yeah!" response from many women to ending the dyeing charade. As the months of the original lockdown wound down and businesses began to open back up, I wondered what the move would be. Would women automatically return to the cover-up routine, or had a shift happened? Imagine my exultation when multiple news articles appeared that not only reported the latter but showcased it with exquisite photo essays capturing women of various ages, colors, and circumstances, transitioning to their natural gray, some just beginning, some midway there, some completely transformed. I was gladdened when actress Andie MacDowell made a stir on the red carpet at Cannes rocking her silver; I cheered even louder for the brave women closer to me—my sister, a friend, a neighbor, a grocery store clerk—who dared to make the same choice. So many beautiful souls growing into the gray. I love it.

Other women weren't the only ones growing in this realm during the pandemic. I did too, just in a different way. Over the course of my lifetime, I've worn my hair many ways, most recently, for more than a decade, cut very short, and in the last couple of years before COVID, I was garnering a noticeably increasing number of positive comments on it from friends and strangers alike. A fact I found not only interesting but also ironic, considering I was now at a point in my life—in the wake of my defining moment and the early stages of trauma healing—when I couldn't care less what others thought about my appearance. At the same time that more praise for my hair was coming at me from the outside, I was aware of a vague sense of unhappiness with it—the style anyway—building inside me. And when the pandemic came along, it provided the perfect laboratory for excavating both the fullness and the source of my creeping dissatisfaction.

While the salon shutdown during quarantine didn't keep me from coloring my hair, like for so many women, it did prevent me from getting it cut as frequently as I'd become accustomed to. Instead of trimming my inch-long layers every six weeks, months and months passed as they lengthened into softer waves, framing my face in a way faintly but fondly remembered from long ago. Liking what I saw in the mirror, I began to toy with growing out my hair. But something about that idea felt so uncomfortable that as soon as there was a relaxation in the pandemic health and safety restrictions in the fall of 2020, I booked an appointment and got it all chopped off, anticipating relief. Instead, I felt an odd sort of regret. Confused, I repeated that pattern twice more, the regret growing stronger each time until finally it dawned on me what I was battling: appearance shame, of a different stripe perhaps, but at its core the very same dynamic that I'd written about in my first chapter.

I could feel only incredibly sheepish and then laugh at myself when I unearthed what was at the bottom of my struggle, an old message lurking in the depths of my subconscious: "Older women with gray hair should not wear it long." From an early age, I'd heard that message loud and clear, over and over, from my mother and her peers. It was one of their generation's inviolable "beauty laws," of which there were many. And it had obviously sunk into the abyss of my psyche and was still informing my way of being in the world. Not having consciously thought of it for eons, I'd had absolutely no clue how it had been quietly operating in me and powerfully shaping my behavior, behind-the-scenes. Once I brought it out into the open, however, it was easy to let it go. It doesn't belong to me. It doesn't line up with my core values, my sense of who I am, and how I want to show up in the world. It's just the most recent example of early programming that doesn't serve me, so it's out of here.

Starting in January 2021, I began to grow out my hair, and who knows how long I'll let it get—maybe down to my ass, though I doubt it. At some point, too, I suppose I might feel like chopping it all off again, though I suspect that might not be for quite a while yet. The thing is, whatever I decide, I hope it'll be because I—my core self, the truest me—want to do it, not because some unconscious tape from long ago is driving me unaware. Anyway, it's been nine months now, and I'm delighting in my already ampler waves of gray. They bring me great pleasure as I move another degree closer to personal authenticity in this moment, to growing into the gray. Good heavens, it's a lifetime's work, isn't it? But infinitely liberating.

I leave you now with a quote from Kristi Nelson, the executive director of A Network for Grateful Living, because it sums up the direction that all of us—I, you, this nation, the world—are being called to head in and because it seems so very timely. She says, "The path forward may sometimes be unclear. And it may be messy. But the shared heart is calling, and we have an opportunity to make lasting shifts toward love and justice in our world." Here's to each of us grabbing this opportunity and giving it our all, each in our own crazy, marvelous, unique way, for our blessed individual and collective good.

ACKNOWLEDGMENTS

Sometimes our light goes out but is blown again into flame by an
encounter with another human being. Each of us owes the deepest
thanks to those who have rekindled this inner light.
—*Albert Schweitzer*

It's time for me to offer my deepest thanks to those who have
rekindled my flame, and I do so with a full heart, near to overflowing with how richly blessed I am by the people who surround
me. Instead of saving him for "last but not least," as seems common, I begin with my husband, Rick Davidson. Thank you for
loving me steadfastly and for letting me return the gift. This book
would not exist without you. You are a rock upon which I have
found safety, support, and solace amidst the tempests of life. May
I be the wind beneath your wings as you now retire from the
workaday world and explore your own next chapter. My son, Eric
Davidson, comes next. Thank you for volunteering to come to
Earth to help me heal. Without the experience of birthing, raising,
and walking alongside you on the trauma road—at first unconsciously, now awake—teaching each other and learning as we go,
I wouldn't be where I am today. Your loving nature and innate

wisdom inform these pages—more than you'll ever know. My last family nod goes to Leslie Wertam, dear sister of mine. Thank you for being there, from the beginning, and for holding me in love through it all. It has not escaped my awareness that as first child you may have borne the brunt of our family's pain and, if not for you, my story might be a good deal uglier.

In thinking specifically about writing, I immediately recall an undergraduate professor, Dr. Searing, who is likely now deceased, so I fling these words for her out into the ether. Thank you for being the first person to tell me that I had something interesting to say and a unique way of saying it. If I'd had the capacity to trust you or myself back then, my first book would have been published forty years ago, but I'm glad that some wise part of myself tucked your vision of author me away in my heart and kept it safe until now. Equally immediately, but much more currently, I think of Linda Fogerson. Thank you for taking a chance on hiring me into a grant writing position for which I had no qualifications (save that "academic pedigree" you so relentlessly reminded me of and insisted I not squander), for believing in me when I didn't believe in myself, and for the opportunity to reignite my love of playing with words.

I first started to embrace *writer* as a self-descriptor because of two fellow 5Rhythms fanatics, authors both. Anne Randerson, thank you for your deep insights into the writer's life, your ardent affirmation of my initial steps onto its path, and your ongoing coaching as I continue walking it. Elizabeth Fee, thank you for your ready willingness to review multiple versions of this work and for your wise feedback that both applauded my efforts and lovingly challenged me to grow in the craft. I adore dancing through life with both of you!

Finally, the person who helped me to stand fully upright in the reality of being a writer is Nirmala Nataraj, editor extraordinaire.

Thank you for your enthusiasm about my voice, your affirmation of my abilities, your belief in the importance of my message, and your support along the journey toward publishing. Your insightful suggestions, gentle yet probing critique, astonishing vision, and uncanny ability to understand where I was going, even when I didn't, are precious gifts, the impact of which I am only just beginning to grasp. I'm so very glad I found you, and I look forward to working with you on future projects.

Long ago, I heard an author—can't remember whom now—say that on the way to producing a book, writing is the easy part. I remember scoffing at the idea, but I'm not scoffing any longer. There's so much more to the process than I ever imagined, and I find I'm now living the truth of the phrase, "It takes a village." Nicole White, publishing assistant, thank you for being wise beyond your years as well as game to enter territory new to us both, and for your diligent help with the permissions, bibliography, and resources. Continue to work on your own writing, and someday you'll be the one birthing a book. Karin Blair, beta reader, thank you for carving out time in your very busy life to give this first-time author your honest feedback, helpful suggestions, and kind encouragement, and for sharing reflections on your own heroine's journey, all of which enriched both this book and me.

For assistance navigating the unknown waters of publishing, I turned to the fine folks at kn literary arts. At the helm of my ship, there was the gifted Elisabeth Rinaldi. Thank you for keeping this book on course with your extraordinary expertise, and for keeping me from getting swamped by the sometimes choppy seas of first-time experience. (I think therapist should be part of your job title.) In addition, thank you for copyediting this work with such a keen eye, saving me from, among other things, occasionally drowning my readers in over-lengthy sentences. You helped me grow into being an author and made it so much fun along the way. kn literary also blessed me with Erin Seaward-Hiatt, book designer. Thank you for bringing *Growing into the Gray* alive with your vision and deftness. And Audra Figgins, proofreader, thank you for your exacting attention to detail. I'm grateful to have sailed with this capable crew.

Many other people less directly related to the writing and production of *Growing into the Gray* were still integral to its creation. Livia Walsh, thank you for being compassion-personified and for walking the talk of mindful living with such stunning grace. I'm grateful you didn't actually disappear once our therapy was done because your continued presence in my life through your weekly meditation group was such a blessing to me. Kristy Arbon, thank you for lessons in embodiment, trusting emergence, how to be a good animal, and much more over the years. During the earliest months of COVID, you and the online Graduates' Journey community provided a much-needed safe haven and a launching pad for my creativity.

Christina Graham-Smith, thank you, from one *lyrical* gal to another, for the vulnerability, authenticity, and vibrancy with which you teach. You and your 5Rhythms classes have given me roots and wings. Lucia Horan, thank you for being the embodiment of courage and *flow*, and for taking me deep, deep, deep into the mysteries and power of the dance. You are a beacon guiding so many of us home.

Elaine Dodge, thank you for getting it all going with your gift of Mark Nepo's *The Book of Awakening* upon my "retirement," for hearing and seeing me on a level few do, and for freely sharing your earthly and inner treasures with me—providing me with literal and figurative refuge. Sheila Walker, thank you for many years of abiding friendship and support, and for weekly "walking and talking" during COVID, where we discussed solving the problems of the world, and I first began to speak of myself as a writer. Karen

Hohlweck, thank you, fellow trauma thriver, for your honesty, open heart, and willingness to talk about it all, and for your loving company as we both venture forth into new vocations. Deborah White, thank you for more things than can ever be adequately expressed here, but especially for being my BFF and the one who kept me from going over that second brink. I'm glad that I could return the favor, in a way, and that we're now exploring the big, beautiful world of post-traumatic growth together.

Finally, to my Swimmin' Women, Vivian Sayward (whose genius at loving connection brought me back to the ocean and nudges me forth into greater depths), Judith Coates (whose brilliance continually opens my eyes and heart to the wonders of life—marine and terrestrial), and Rachel Kowalski (whose buoyant nature keeps me afloat both in and out of the water). Thank you for our sacred Saturday mornings in the salty sea and for holding me in your hearts during my long dry spell.

In truly twenty-first-century style, I wish to give thanks to cyberspace. Through various online learning communities during my recovery, the internet brought many wonderful people into my life, three of whom proved to be especially important to my personal process, and thus this book. Mac Hudson, thank you for your astonishingly compassionate heart and audacious commitment to practicing unconditional love, for your willingness to share learnings from your conscious uncoupling and subsequent reopening to intimate partnership, and for soulful hikes in the Sonoran Desert. Lisa Sattell, thank you for your inspiringly open spirit, for your willingness to share the story of your own painful traumas, for your ongoing work to embody self-love and feminine power, and for twice coming from the Midwest to play with me here in SoCal. Valerie Perkins, thank you for your boundless curiosity; for your willingness to integrate your past, make sense of your present, and build a bright future for yourself and others;

and for showing up every month, going on over three years now, for our beloved one-on-one Zoom sessions. I never imagined that I could feel so much love for and so close to and supported by someone I've yet to meet in person.

Finally, I wish to acknowledge my dedicatee, Gloria Gonzalez. Thank you for being you, for giving yourself so wholeheartedly to the project of my recovery from trauma, and for being my doula as I conceived, gestated, and gave birth to this book. The *I Ching* says, "Genius is the ability to receive from the Universe." To me, you are the embodiment of that definition of genius, the clearest channel of Love I have ever encountered, plugged into Source Wisdom in a way that transcends most mortals' experience, yet ever abiding in humility and compassion. It takes my breath away to ponder my good fortune in being led to you, and there are probably not enough days left to me to adequately pay forward what you have given me. But I'm going to try.

RESOURCES

Should you wish to dig deeper into some of the ideas raised in this book, I've listed a variety of resources that I've had varying levels of direct experience with—some before I wrote these essays, some during, and some not until after I had finished writing and was preparing the manuscript for publication. All are pertinent to or provocative of the themes I touched on, begging for inclusion. Since I'm a voracious reader, my exploration into any subject almost always begins with a book; only after do I move to cyberspace. Many of the listings here reflect that movement, going from title to author to website, hopefully giving you enough information to follow your own preferred route of investigation. As I divided up the material to aid your search, I realized that many of these resources speak to more than one topic. I did my best to place each of them in a category that reflected what I thought was its main thrust. (Any possible misalignment is entirely my doing.) Enjoy exploring, and may you find what you need.

Regarding trauma specifically, the good news for everyone is that recovery from it—just like pretty much everything in life—is not a one-size-fits-all prospect. Thankfully, there are so many ways now—especially in our digital age—of making contact and joining with others in transforming the wounds to body-mind-spirit that trauma inflicts, and while more are still sorely needed, a good number address the critical issues pertaining to specific populations and are low cost or even no-cost. After perusing this list, which is reflective of *my* journey, I invite you to see what other tools, guides, and supports you can find that resonate—perhaps more strongly—with *you*, wherever you are on your own healing path.

Trauma

Waking the Tiger: Healing Trauma and *In an Unspoken Voice: How the Body Releases Trauma and Restores Goodness*, Peter A. Levine, somaticexperiencing.com

The Body Keeps the Score: Brain, Mind, and Body in the Healing of Trauma, Bessel van der Kolk, besselvanderkolk.com

How to Do the Work: Recognize Your Patterns, Heal from Your Past, and Create Your Self, Nicole LePera, theholisticpsychologist.com

Healing Collective Trauma: A Process for Integrating Our Intergenerational and Cultural Wounds, Thomas Hübl, thomashuebl.com

It Didn't Start with You: How Inherited Family Trauma Shapes Who We Are and How to End the Cycle, Mark Wolynn, markwolynn.com

Trauma: The Invisible Epidemic: How Trauma Works and How We Can Heal from It, Paul Conti, drpaulconti.com

What Happened to You?: Conversations on Trauma, Resilience, and Healing, Bruce D. Perry and Oprah Winfrey, bdperry.com, oprah.com

Somatic Experiencing International, traumahealing.org

Organic Intelligence, organicintelligence.org

The Wisdom of Trauma, a movie featuring Gabor Maté,
thewisdomoftrauma.com

Mindfulness and Compassion

*Full Catastrophe Living: Using the Wisdom of Your Body and Mind to
Face Stress, Pain, and Illness*, Jon Kabat-Zinn, mindfulnesscds.com

*A Fierce Heart: Finding Strength, Courage, and Wisdom in Any
Moment*, Spring Washam, springwasham.com

*Altered Traits: Science Reveals How Meditation Changes Your Mind,
Brain, and Body*, Daniel Goleman and Richard J. Davidson,
danielgoleman.info, richardjdavidson.com

*Trauma-Sensitive Mindfulness: Practices for Safe and Transforma-
tive Healing*, David A. Treleaven, davidtreleaven.com

Stay Woke: A Meditation Guide for the Rest of Us, Justin Michael
Williams, justinmichaelwilliams.com

Self-Compassion: The Proven Power of Being Kind to Yourself, Kristin
Neff, self-compassion.org

*The Mindful Path to Self-Compassion: Freeing Yourself from Destructive
Thoughts and Emotions*, Christopher K. Germer, chrisgermer.com

*The Mindful Self-Compassion Workbook: A Proven Way to Accept
Yourself, Build Inner Strength, and Thrive*, Kristin Neff and
Christopher K. Germer

Center for Mindful Self-Compassion, centerformsc.org

Somatic Self-Compassion, kristyarbon.com

UC San Diego Center for Mindfulness, cih.ucsd.edu/mindfulness

SOMATICS, MIND-BODY PRACTICES

Maps to Ecstasy: A Healing Journey for the Untamed Spirit and
Sweat Your Prayers: Movement as Spiritual Practice, Gabrielle
Roth, 5rhythms.com, ravenrecording.com

Daring to Rest: Reclaim Your Power with Yoga Nidra Rest Meditation,
Karen Brody, daringtorest.com

Radian Rest: Yoga Nidra for Deep Relaxation and Awakened Clarity, Tracee Stanley, radiantrest.com

*Bodyfulness: Somatic Practices for Presence, Empowerment, and
Waking Up in This Life*, Christine Caldwell, naropa.academia.
edu/ChristineCaldwell

*Awareness through Movement: Easy-to-Do Health Exercises to
Improve Your Posture, Vision, Imagination, and Personal Awareness*, Moshé Feldenkrais, feldenkrais.com

Mind & Body: Mental Exercises for Physical Wellbeing; Physical Exercises for Mental Wellbeing, The School of Life, theschooloflife.com

*Bouncing Back: Rewiring Your Brain for Maximum Resilience and
Well-Being*, Linda Graham, lindagraham-mft.net

*Anchored: How to Befriend Your Nervous System Using Polyvagal
Theory*, Deb Dana, rhythmofregulation.com

5Rhythms, luciahoran.com, shakingspiritwaves.com, christina5rhythms.com, thecitywaves.com, jenellemsmith.com

Azul, pathofazul.com

Open Floor, openfloor.org

ZeroOne, inzero.one

Nia, nianow.com

Yoga Nidra, irest.org

Feldenkrais Method, anoone.org

The Non-Linear Movement Method, michaelaboehm.com/the -non-linear-movement-method-2

RACIAL JUSTICE

How to Be an Antiracist, Ibram X. Kendi, ibramxkendi.com

The Inner Work of Racial Justice: Healing Ourselves and Transforming Our Communities Through Mindfulness, Rhonda V. Magee, rhondavmagee.com

Biased: Uncovering the Hidden Prejudice That Shapes What We See, Think, and Do, Jennifer L. Eberhardt, web.stanford .edu/~eberhard/about-jennifer-eberhardt

White Fragility: Why It's So Hard for White People to Talk About Racism, Robin DiAngelo, robindiangelo.com

My Grandmother's Hands: Racialized Trauma and the Pathway to Mending Our Hearts and Bodies, Resmaa Menakem, resmaa.com

Me and White Supremacy: Combat Racism, Change the World, and Become a Good Ancestor, Layla F. Saad, laylafsaad.com

See No Stranger: A Memoir and Manifesto of Revolutionary Love, Valarie Kaur, valariekaur.com/revolutionary-love-project

Healing: The Act of Radical Self Care, Joi Lewis, joiunlimited.com

SEXUALITY

Come as You Are: The Surprising New Science That Will Transform Your Sex Life, Emily Nagoski, emilynagoski.com

Mating in Captivity: Unlocking Erotic Intelligence, Esther Perel, estherperel.com

Why Good Sex Matters: Understanding the Neuroscience of Pleasure for a Smarter, Happier, and More Purpose-Filled Life, Nan Wise, askdoctornan.com

The New Art of Sexual Ecstasy: Following the Path of Sacred Sexuality, Margot Anand, margotanand.com

The Sexual Healing Journey: A Guide for Survivors of Sexual Abuse, Wendy Maltz, healthysex.com

Better Than I Ever Expected: Straight Talk About Sex After Sixty, Joan Price, joanprice.com

RAINN (Rape, Abuse & Incest National Network), rainn.org

National Sexual Violence Resource Center, nsvrc.org

Alternative/Integrative Medicine, Health, and Well-Being

Mind Over Medicine: Scientific Proof That You Can Heal Yourself, Lissa Rankin, lissarankin.com

When the Body Says No: Understanding the Stress-Disease Connection, Gabor Maté, drgabormate.com

The Angel and the Assassin: The Tiny Brain Cell That Changed the Course of Medicine, Donna Jackson Nakazawa, donnajacksonnakazawa.com

Ayurveda Lifestyle Wisdom: A Complete Prescription to Optimize Your Health, Prevent Disease, and Live with Vitality and Joy, Acharya Shunya, acharyashunya.com

Healing Ourselves: Biofield Science and the Future of Health, Shamini Jain, shaminijain.com

Lost Connections: Uncovering the Real Causes of Depression—And the Unexpected Solutions, Johann Hari, thelostconnections.com

The Chopra Center, chopra.com

The Center for Mind-Body Medicine, cmbm.org

Consciousness and Healing Initiative (CHI), chi.is

University of Arizona, Andrew Weil Center for Integrative Medicine, integrativemedicine.arizona.edu

Omkar Ayurveda, omkarayurveda.com

Personal and Planetary Transformation

A Network for Grateful Living, gratefulness.org

Greater Good Science Center, ggsc.berkeley.edu

Science & Nonduality (SAND), scienceandnonduality.com

Esalen Institute, esalen.org

The Fetzer Institute, fetzer.org

Mind & Life Institute, mindandlife.org

HeartMath Institute, heartmath.org

I AM The Medicine, eightelementswest.com/i-am-the-medicine

BIBLIOGRAPHY

Allen, Summer. "Positive Neuroscience." *Greater Good Science Center*, February 2019.

Anand, Margot. *The Art of Everyday Ecstasy: The Seven Tantric Keys for Bringing Passion, Spirit, and Joy into Every Part of Your Life*. New York, NY: Harmony, 2015.

Angelou, Maya. "Love Liberates". Youtube video, 5:34. March 4, 2013. www.youtube.com/watch?v=cbecKv2xR14.

Applewhite, Ashton. *This Chair Rocks: A Manifesto Against Ageism*. New York, NY: Celadon Books, 2016.

Barks, Coleman, trans. *The Essential Rumi*. New York, NY: HarperCollins Publishers, 2004.

Boehm, Michaela. *The Wild Woman's Way: Unlock Your Full Potential for Pleasure, Power, and Fulfillment*. New York, NY: Enliven, 2018.

Brackett, Marc. *Permission to Feel: Unlocking the Power of Emotions to Help Our Kids, Ourselves, and Our Society Thrive*. New York, NY: Celadon Books, 2019.

Brainpicker. "Malcolm Gladwell on Changing Your Mind." Soundcloud audio, 5:57. 2015. soundcloud.com/brainpicker/malcolm-gladwell-on-changing-your-mind.

Brody, Karen. *Daring to Rest: Reclaim Your Power with Yoga Nidra Rest Medita.* Boulder, CO: Sounds True, 2017.

Brown, Margaret Wise. *Mister Dog: The Dog Who Belonged to Himself.* New York, NY: Golden Books, 2003.

Caldwell, Christine. *Bodyfulness: Somatic Practices for Presence, Empowerment, and Waking Up in This Life.* Boulder, CO: Shambhala Publications, 2018.

Carucci, Eleanor. "Silver Linings." *New Yorker*, June 4, 2021. www.newyorker.com/culture/photo-booth/the-unexpected-beauty-of-covid-hair.

"CDC-Kaiser ACE Study." Centers for Disease Control and Prevention. April 06, 2021. www.cdc.gov/violenceprevention/aces/about.html?CDC_AA_refVal=https://www.cdc.gov/violenceprevention/acestudy/about.html.

Church, Dawson. *Bliss Brain: The Neuroscience of Remodeling Your Brain for Resilience, Creativity, and Joy.* Carlsbad, CA: Hay House, 2020.

Collier, Lorna. "Growth After Trauma." *American Psychological Association*, vol. 47, no. 10 (November 2016). www.apa.org/monitor/2016/11/growth-trauma.

Corn, Seane. *Revolution of the Soul: Awaken to Love Through Raw Truth, Radical Healing, and Conscious Action.* Boulder, CO: Sounds True, 2019.

DiAngelo, Robin. *White Fragility: Why It's So Hard for White People to Talk About Racism.* New York, NY: Beacon Press, 2018.

Eberhardt, Jennifer L. *Biased: Uncovering the Hidden Prejudice That Shapes What We See, Think, and Do.* New York, NY: Viking, 2019.

Felitti, Vincent, Robert F. Anda, Dale Nordenberg, David F. Williamson, Alison M. Spitz, Valerie Edwards, Mary P. Koss, and James S. Marks. "Relationship of Childhood Abuse and Household Dysfunction to Many of the Leading Causes of Death in Adults: The Adverse Childhood Experiences (ACE) Study." *American Journal of Preventative Medicine.* April 2019. www.ajpmonline.org/article/S0749-3797(19)30143-6/fulltext.

Gates, Melinda. *The Movement of Lift: How Empowering Women Changes the World.* Sydney: Macmillan Australia, 2019.

Germer, Christopher K. *The Mindful Path to Self-Compassion: Freeing Yourself from Destructive Thoughts and Emotions.* New York, NY: Guilford Press, 2009.

Gilbert, Elizabeth. *Big Magic: Creative Living Beyond Fear.* New York, NY: Riverhead Books, 2015.

Goleman, Daniel, and Richard J. Davidson. *Altered Traits: Science Reveals How Meditation Changes Your Mind, Brain, and Body.* New York, NY: Avery, 2017.

Graham, Linda. *Bouncing Back: Rewiring Your Brain for Maximum Resilience and Well-Being.* Novato, CA: New World Library, 2013.

Hanh, Thich Nhat. *No Mud, No Lotus: The Art of Transforming Suffering.* Berkeley, CA: Parallax Press, 2014.

Hari, Johann. *Lost Connections: Uncovering the Real Causes of Depression*—And *the Unexpected Solutions.* London: Bloomsbury USA, 2018.

Johnson, Natalie. "These Women Embraced Their Gray Hair During Covid. Now They're Never Going Back." NBCNews.com. September 21, 2021. www.nbcnews.com/know-your-value/feature/these-women-embraced-their-gray-hair-during-covid-now-they-ncna1279718.

Judkis, Maura. "Some Young Women Embraced Their Gray Hair During the Pandemic. They Might Not Go Back." *The Washington Post.* April 12, 2021. www.washingtonpost.com/lifestyle/style/gray-hair-young-pandemic-look/2021/04/11/2c5ce9ac-90bd-11eb-9668-89be11273c09_story.html.

Kabat-Zinn, Jon. *Full Catastrophe Living: Using the Wisdom of Your Body and Mind to Face Stress, Pain, and Illness.* New York, NY: Bantam Books, 2013.

———. *Wherever You Go There You Are: Mindfulness Meditation in Everyday Life.* New York, NY: Hachette Books, 2014.

Kendi, Ibram X. *How to Be an Antiracist.* New York, NY: One World, 2019.

Levine, Peter A. *In An Unspoken Voice: How the Body Releases Trauma and Restores Goodness.* Berkeley, CA: North Atlantic Books, 2010.

Levine, Peter A., and Ann Frederick. *Waking the Tiger: Healing Trauma.* Berkeley, CA: North Atlantic Books, 1997.

Magee, Rhonda V. *The Inner Work of Racial Justice: Healing Ourselves and Transforming Our Communities Through Mindfulness.* New York, NY: TarcherPerigree, 2019.

Maté, Gabor. *When the Body Says No: Understanding the Stress-Disease Connection.* Hoboken, NJ: John Wiley & Sons, 2003.

McLaren, Karla. *The Language of Emotions: What Your Feelings Are Trying to Tell You.* Boulder, CO: Sounds True, 2010.

Menigoz, Wendy, Tracy T. Latz, Robin A. Ely, Cimone Kamei, Gregory Melvin, and Drew Sinatra. "Integrative and Lifestyle Medicine Strategies Should Include Earthing (Grounding): Review of Research Evidence and Clinical Observations." ScienceDirect. November 14, 2019. www.sciencedirect.com/science/article/pii/S1550830719305476.

Murdock, Maureen. *The Heroine's Journey: Woman's Quest for Wholeness.* Boston, MA: Shambhala Publications, 1990.

Nagoski, Emily. *Come as You Are: The Surprising New Science That Will Transform Your Sex Life.* New York, NY: Simon & Schuster Paperbacks, 2015.

Neff, Kristin. *Self-Compassion: The Proven Power of Being Kind to Yourself.* New York, NY: William Morrow, 2015.

Neff, Kristin, and Christopher Germer. *The Mindful Self-Compassion Workbook: A Proven Way to Accept Yourself, Build Inner Strength, and Thrive.* New York, NY: Guilford Press, 2018.

Nelson, Kristi, and David Steindl-Rast. *Everyday Gratitude: Inspiration for Living Life as a Gift.* North Adams, MA: Storey Publishing, 2018.

Nepo, Mark. *The Book of Awakening: Having the Life You Want by Being Present to the Life You Have.* San Francisco, CA: Conari Press, 2011.

Oliver, Mary. *New and Selected Poems: Volume One.* Boston, MA: Beacon Press, 1992.

Orloff, Judith. *The Empath's Survival Guide: Life Strategies for Sensitive People.* Boulder, CO: Sounds True, 2018.

Oschman, James L., Gaétan Chevalier, and Richard Brown. "The Effects of Grounding (Earthing) on Inflammation, the Immune Response, Wound Healing, and Prevention and Treatment of Chronic Inflammatory and Autoimmune Diseases." *Journal of Inflammation Research.* March 24, 2015. www.ncbi.nlm.nih.gov/pmc/articles/PMC4378297/.

Peck, M. Scott. *The Road Less Traveled: A New Psychology of Love, Traditional Values and Spiritual Growth.* New York, NY. Simon & Schuster, 2002.

Perel, Esther. *Mating in Captivity: Unlocking Erotic Intelligence.* New York, NY: HarperCollins Publishers, 2006.

———. "The Secret to Desire in a Long-Term Relationship." Youtube video, 19:10, February 14, 2013. www.youtube.com/watch?v=sa0RUmGTCYY.

Porges, Seth. "The Polyvagal Theory: The New Science of Safety and Trauma." Youtube video, 28:09, November 3, 2017. www.youtube.com/watch?v=br8-qebjIgs&t=13s.

Porges, Stephen W. *The Pocket Guide to the Polyvagal Theory: The Transformative Power of Feeling Safe.* New York, NY: W.W. Norton & Company, 2017.

"Preventing Adverse Childhood Experiences." Centers for Disease Control and Prevention. April 6, 2021. www.cdc.gov/violenceprevention/acestudy/fastfact.html?CDC_AA_refVal=https:%2; www.cdc.gov/violenceprevention/childabuseandneglect/aces/fastfact.html.

Rankin, Lissa. *Mind Over Medicine: Scientific Proof That You Can Heal Yourself.* Carlsbad, CA: Hay House, 2020.

Roth, Gabrielle. *Connections: Threads of Intuitive Wisdom.* New York, NY: Raven Recording, 2014.

———. *Sweat Your Prayers: Movement as Spiritual Practice.* New York, NY: Penguin Putnam, 1997.

Roth, Gabrielle, and John Loudon. *Maps to Ecstasy: A Healing Journey for the Untamed Spirit.* Novato, CA: Nataraj Publishing, 1998.

Saint-Laurent, Roger, and Sharlene Bird. "Somatic Experiencing: How Trauma Can Be Overcome." *Psychology Today.* March 26, 2015. www.psychologytoday.com/us/blog/the-intelligent-divorce/201503/somatic-experiencing.

Segal, Zindel V., J. Mark G. Williams, and John D. Teasdale. *Mindfulness-Based Cognitive Therapy for Depression: A New Approach to Preventing Relapse.* New York, NY: Guilford Press, 2002.

Seuss, Dr. *Horton Hears a Who!* New York, NY: Random House Children's Books, 1954.

Shaw, Miranda. *Passionate Enlightenment: Women in Tantric Buddhism.* Princeton, NJ: Princeton University Press, 2021.

Shunya, Acharya. *Ayurveda Lifestyle Wisdom: A Complete Prescription to Optimize Your Health, Prevent Disease, and Live with Vitality and Joy.* Boulder, CO: Sounds True, 2017.

Singh, Kathleen Dowling. *The Grace in Aging: Awaken As You Grow Older.* Somerville, MA: Wisdom Publications, 2014.

"Subtle Energy & Biofield Healing: Evidence, Practice, & Future Directions." Consciousness and Healing Initiative, February 2020. www.chi.is/wp-content/uploads/2020/01/CHI_Systems_Mapping_Report_1_2020_V2.pdf.

Thomas, Katherine Woodward. *Conscious Uncoupling: 5 Steps to Living Happily Even After, How to Break Up in a Whole New Way.* New York, NY: Harmony Books, 2015.

Treleaven, David A. *Trauma-Sensitive Mindfulness: Practices for Safe and Transformative Healing.* New York, NY: W.W Norton & Company, 2018.

Walker, Alice. "An Evening with Alice Walker—Writer's Symposium by the Sea 2020." UCSDTV video, 1:22:32, March 24, 2020. www.ucsd.tv/shows/An-Evening-with-Alice-Walker-Writers-Symposium-by-the-Sea-2020-35143.

van der Kolk, Bessel. *The Body Keeps the Score: Brain, Mind, and Body in the Healing of Trauma.* New York, NY: Penguin Books, 2015.

Wise, Nan. *Why Good Sex Matters: Understanding the Neuroscience of Pleasure for a Smarter, Happier, and More Purpose-Filled Life.* New York, NY: Houghton Mifflin Harcourt, 2020.

Zucker, Martin, Gaetan Chevalier, and Clint Ober. "Grounding the Human Body: The Healing Benefits of Earthing." Chopra. September 07, 2019. chopra.com/articles/grounding-the-human-body-the-healing-benefits-of-earthing.

ABOUT THE AUTHOR

Laurie Lee Davidson has always loved a challenge, which explains why this book exists. When a publishing insider told her that no one will read a collection of essays unless the author is a known entity, it was all she needed to hear. Not a celebrity, Davidson believes we *all* have compelling stories and insights to share, and that in the sharing, we heal ourselves and each other. As she sees it, this is the whole reason we're here on this planet.

Born in 1958, she spent her formative years on the Eastern Seaboard of the United States, migrated through other gorgeous parts of the country, and finally settled in Southern California twenty-five years ago. While grateful for her fine formal education, Davidson more highly prizes the knowledge and wisdom she gains through curiosity and a commitment to lifelong learning. Vocationally, she explored diverse fields, never really finding her "thing," though writing was a constant. It wasn't until COVID-19 struck that she realized a book was inside her, just waiting to get out. This is her first one. Stay tuned for others.

When she's not playing with words or moving to music, she can most often be found communing with family and friends, immersed in the nearest body of water, or with her nose in a book. Connect with her at laurieleedavidson.com.